PENGUIN TWENTIETH-CENTURY CLASSICS

THE WASTE LAND AND OTHER POEMS

Thomas Stearns Eliot was born in St. Louis, Missouri, on September 26, 1888, and educated at Harvard, the Sorbonne, and Oxford. He settled in England in 1914 and married Vivian Haigh-Wood in 1915. He worked for a City of London bank while writing poetry, teaching, and reviewing. He was soon recognized as a force in the British literary world. *The Sacred Wood*, a collection of critical essays, was well received, and in 1922 he founded a new journal, *The Criterion*, which had an intellectual influence far greater than its small circulation might suggest. *The Waste Land*, which confirmed his reputation as an innovative poet, appeared in the first issue of *The Criterion*. In 1925 he became a director of the publishing firm Faber and Faber, and in that capacity controlled the firm's poetry list during its years of preeminence. In 1927 he became a British subject and a member of the Church of England, describing himself in 1928 as "classical in literature, royalist in politics, and Anglo-Catholic in religion." His verse thereafter has a strong devotional aspect, and the crown of his achievement as a poet was *Four Quartets* (1935–1942), but his interests had also turned to the theatre. The unfinished *Sweeney Agonistes* (1932) was an experiment of great originality. Later he wrote *Murder in the Cathedral* (1935), designed for an ecclesiastical setting, and then a sequence of verse plays for the secular theatre: *The Family Reunion* (1939), *The Cocktail Party* (1950), *The Confidential Clerk* (1954), and *The Elder Statesman* (1959).

Eliot visited the United States in 1932–1933 as Charles Eliot Norton Professor of Poetry at Harvard; his lectures were published as *The Use of Poetry and the Use of Criticism* (1933). His departure from London signified the virtual end of his marriage. His wife died in 1947 after many years of mental disturbance. In 1948 he was awarded the Nobel Prize for Literature, and in that year published *Notes Towards a Definition of Culture*. He married Valerie Fletcher in 1957. Though he was often ill he continued to write, and collections of his essays appeared at intervals, the last being *To Criticize the Critic* (1965). He died in January 1965.

*   *   *

Born in 1919 and educated at Liverpool University, Frank Kermode served in the Royal Navy from 1940 to 1946, and after the war was a lecturer at Durham and Reading universities before holding chairs at Manchester, Bristol, University College, London, and Cambridge. He was Charles Eliot Norton Professor at Harvard for 1977–1978, and has been a visiting professor at Columbia, Yale, Wesleyan, and other American universities. The author of many critical works, he has also written the memoir *Not Entitled* (Farrar, Straus and Giroux, 1995).

THE WASTE LAND
AND OTHER POEMS

T. S. ELIOT

EDITED BY
FRANK KERMODE

PENGUIN BOOKS

PENGUIN BOOKS

Published by the Penguin Group

Penguin Putnam Inc., 375 Hudson Street,
New York, New York 10014, U.S.A.

Penguin Books Ltd, 27 Wrights Lane, London W8 5TZ, England

Penguin Books Australia Ltd, Ringwood, Victoria, Australia

Penguin Books Canada Ltd, 10 Alcorn Avenue,
Toronto, Ontario, Canada M4V 3B2

Penguin Books (N.Z.) Ltd, 182–190 Wairau Road,
Auckland 10, New Zealand

Penguin Books Ltd, Registered Offices:
Harmondsworth, Middlesex, England

This volume first published in Penguin Books 1998

1 3 5 7 9 10 8 6 4 2

LIBRARY OF CONGRESS CATALOGING-IN-PUBLICATION DATA
Eliot, T. S. (Thomas Stearns), 1888–1965.
The waste land and other poems / T. S. Eliot ; edited by Frank
Kermode.
p.   cm.—(Penguin twentieth-century classics)
Includes bibliographical references.
ISBN 0 14 11.8072 2 (pbk.)
I. Kermode, Frank, 1919–   .   II. Title.   III. Series.
PS3509.L43W385   1998
821'.912—dc21   97–34618

Printed in the United States of America
Set in Bembo

CONTENTS

INTRODUCTION

T. S. Eliot visited London briefly in 1911 but did not settle in England until 1914, when he went to study philosophy at Merton College, Oxford, where he hoped to meet and be taught by the philosopher F. H. Bradley; but Bradley was a recluse and remained out of reach. Eliot found Oxford dull and preferred London, though still feeling himself to be a foreigner there (he called himself *metoikos,* Greek for an alien resident in a foreign city). At the time, though he had written some remarkable unpublished poems, he appeared to accept philosophy as his vocation. He had begun his graduate work at Harvard and in 1910 studied in Paris, where he heard and pondered the lectures of the eminent philosopher Henri Bergson. This philosophical career continued awhile; he began to review for philosophy journals, and wrote a thesis on the work of his admired Bradley, which Harvard accepted for the degree. (For various reasons, including the wartime difficulties and dangers of crossing the ocean, he never formally collected it.) The thesis (*Knowledge and Experience in the Philosophy of F. H. Bradley*) was published only in 1964, by which time Eliot had completely abandoned his career as professional philosopher, admitting in his introduction to the book that he no longer understood what he had written half a century earlier. But Bradley had been for some years a potent influence; his philosophy was congenial, partly because his prose style was so admirable, partly because he seemed to argue that "the whole world for each is peculiar and private to that soul"—to quote the passage Eliot used in the notes to *The Waste Land*. Hugh Kenner aptly remarks that this passage "might have been composed by a disciplined Prufrock."[1]

Eliot had written poems as an undergraduate at Harvard, but for his formation as a poet the most important moment of his undergraduate career was his coming, in 1908, upon Arthur Symons's book *The Symbolist Movement in Poetry* (1899). This book, originally entitled *The Decadent Movement in Poetry* (decadence ceased to be fashionable after the Oscar Wilde trials), had an importance beyond its intrinsic merits, for it made available to a wider audience some French poets who had already impressed some in the English avant-garde of the 1890s, many of them very much at home in Paris. Eliot, happening on it a little later, found it a revelation: "[B]ut for having read [Symons's] book, I should not, in the year 1908, have heard of [Jules] Laforgue or [Arthur] Rimbaud; I should probably not have begun to read [Paul] Verlaine; and but for reading Verlaine, I should not have heard of [Tristan] Corbière." And this "revelation," he said, "affected the course of my life."[2] It certainly had a powerful effect on his early poetry, which owes much to Laforgue in particular, and it was still, though less conspicuously, an influence on *The Waste Land*.

Another formative influence was the Jacobean drama— the late plays of Shakespeare and the works of Cyril Tourneur, John Webster, John Ford, and others. About these playwrights Eliot made himself thoroughly well informed; he wrote a series of important essays on them for the *Times Literary Supplement*, which were later reprinted in *The Sacred Wood* and *Selected Essays*. At the same time he became a devoted student of Dante, eventually to prove the most venerated of his masters. And while he was writing these poems he was still an admirer of John Donne. Among more modern writers there was, in addition to the French, Henry James, a *metoikos* greatly admired by Pound as well.

To complete this summary of influences, one needs to add that of Ezra Pound. Pound had been living in London since 1908, and Eliot took an early opportunity to seek him out (September 1914). He became Eliot's adviser and promoter, arranging for the publication of his poems in certain American magazines with which he had connections—magazines that, despite their small circulations, enjoyed considerable literary influence. Equally important, he proved himself to be what the dedication of *The Waste Land* calls him, *il miglior fabbro,* the better or the best craftsman.

Pound had shown an interest in Eliot even before he met him, having been told by Conrad Aiken, a close friend of Eliot's, that "there was a guy at Harvard doing funny stuff."[3] Eliot sent him "Prufrock," which Pound at once called "the best poem I have yet had or seen from an American." He went on to call Eliot "the only American I know who has made what I can call adequate preparation for writing. He has actually trained himself *and* modernized himself *on his own.*"[4] He arranged the publication of "Prufrock," and Eliot, stimulated by this endorsement, began to write verse again. Later it was Pound who suggested Théophile Gautier's *Emaux et Camées* as a model for exercises in a different kind of versification, and Eliot wrote "The Hippopotamus," "Whispers of Immortality," and other poems (all submitted to Pound for comment and correction) in the Gautier manner—concise, elegant, and powerful quatrains. Pound also introduced Eliot to London contemporaries likely to help or interest him, with notable consequences; Eliot made the acquaintance of the poet-philosopher T. E. Hulme, shortly afterward killed in France, whose aesthetic Eliot admired, and established a friendship with Wyndham Lewis, painter, conservative polemicist, poet, and editor. In fact, Pound did much to establish Eliot in London literary society, and his efforts did not stop there. Worried about Eliot's health and his relative poverty, Pound energetically devised and promoted schemes to support him financially.

Pound, then, was probably, in these early years, the most decisive influence on Eliot's poetry, not because he made Eliot write as he did, but because of his extraordinary understanding of what the other man was feeling toward; as Eliot remarked, "He was a marvellous critic because he didn't try to turn you into an imitation of himself. He tried to see what you were trying to do."[5] Pound had a connoisseur's appreciation of poetic rhythm, and he saw that Eliot had the same gift but needed encouragement and advice.

A great deal has been written (much of it by Eliot himself) about the body of ideas that underlies his poetry: for instance, the idea that modern poetry must in the nature of the case be difficult; the notion that we have never recovered from a "dissociation of sensibility" that overtook our culture in the seventeenth century, so that modern poetry must relearn its business from Donne and the Jacobeans, from Dante, the greatest of all vernacular poets, and from the French writers he discovered in his reading of Symons.[6]

But it is important to understand that Eliot's response to poetry was of a more instinctive kind than these studies suggest. In May 1935 he remarked in a letter to Stephen Spender that "you don't really criticize any author to whom you have never surrendered yourself. . . . Even just the bewildering minute counts; you have to give yourself up, and then recover yourself, and the third moment is having something to say, before you have wholly forgotten both surrender and recovery. Of course the self recovered is never the same as the self before it was given."[7] He used the word "surrender" in one of his most revealing essays, "Tradition and the Individual Talent" (1919), where he is talking about the poet's mind "as a receptacle for seizing and storing up numberless feelings, phrases, images, which remain there until all the particles which can unite to form a new compound are present together." The work, the impersonal poem, is then to be written, but that cannot be done till the poet surrenders himself to it.[8]

The expression "bewildering minute" comes from a passage in Tourneur's (or Thomas Middleton's) *The Revenger's Tragedy* (III.v.69–79) which Eliot had earlier quoted twice in his published writings (including "Tradition and the Individual Talent"): "Are lordships sold to maintain ladyships / For the poor benefit of a bewildering minute?" asks Tourneur's Vindice, meditating on the skull of his beloved. The lines are now famous because of Eliot's interest in them (when he first mentions them, in "Tradition and the Individual Talent," he calls them "unfamiliar enough to be regarded with fresh attention").[9] He himself had evidently, on encountering them, had the experience he describes, and that experience seemed encapsulated in the words "bewildering minute." The context is of course sexual; it treats orgasm, which the experience of poetry, Eliot strongly implies, can resemble, as a special kind of enchantment inducing pleasure that is accompanied by loss and even dismay—something quite different from the ordinary pleasures of reading, a difference the French writer Roland Barthes had in mind when he distinguished between the pleasure (*plaisir*) of the text and something analogous to orgasm (*jouissance*).[10] One can observe in this account of the bewildering minute of reading a resemblance to the life experience described in *The Waste Land*: "blood shaking my heart / The awful daring of a moment's surrender . . . By this, and this only, we have existed . . ." (lines 402–5); an experience hardly to be called pleasure, a moment of ecstatic dismay, which is quite different from the perfunctory pleasure of the typist and the house agent's clerk in "The Fire Sermon." And perhaps we can recognize a complementary failure to achieve such a surrender, such a withholding of the self, in the lines "I could not / Speak, and my eyes failed, I was neither / Living nor dead, and I knew nothing" (*The Waste Land*, 38–40).

The "bewildering minute" is further described in Eliot's essay on Dante: "The experience of a poem is the experience both of a moment and of a lifetime. It is very much like our intenser experiences of other human beings. There is a first, or an early moment which is unique, of shock and surprise, even of terror . . . a moment which can never be forgotten, but which is never repeated integrally and yet which would become destitute of significance if it did not survive in a larger whole of experience; which survives inside a deeper and calmer feeling. . . ." Speaking of Dante's visionary encounter—or "sexual experience"—with the young Beatrice, he adds, "I cannot find it incredible that what has happened to others should have happened to Dante with much greater intensity."[11]

The point is that for Eliot, reading as well as writing poetry requires a kind of emotional surrender similar to the surrender made in a moment to another person; one need not know anything about the person, and the poetic surrender may well be made before the reader has understood his text. This may be why he trusted Pound (for whose own verse he did not much care) with the overseeing of his poetry; for, in his own way, Pound held a similar belief. This is one reason why *The Waste Land* is the poem we have, and not the longer work that survives in the manuscripts. Examination of Pound's surgery makes it clear enough that he had little concern for what came to be regarded as the structure of ideas in the poem; he simply cut out whatever lines or words failed to please him, sometimes with ribald comment.

Eliot did not accept all Pound's corrections, but was always grateful for his "maieutic" endeavors. "It was in 1922 that I placed before him in Paris the manuscript of a sprawling, chaotic poem called *The Waste Land* which left his hands, reduced to about half its size, in the form in which it appears in print."[12] He was indeed in Pound's debt throughout the period that culminated in *The Waste Land*. In the end they were poets of different kinds, but they had in common the power to respond—to surrender—and also the power to reject; they were fine readers, with minds prepared for poetry, resolved to make new the poetry of the present by understanding the poetry of the past. And an important quality was the pleasure/dismay that poems could and should provide.

To test one's own experience of the poetry of the past might mean a remapping of its conventional history. When Eliot came across Laforgue he was enchanted by what seemed to him an affinity of temperament, a sort of ironic, dandyish elegance to which he felt that he himself, consciously or not, had aspired. "Prufrock" and "Portrait of a Lady," both written after Eliot's return to Harvard in 1911, are Laforguian poems. Laforgue is not generally considered a major poet, and in a sense it could be said that an unbounded admiration for him depended on assumptions and tastes that had carried over from the nineties—from the milieu of Arthur Symons (who had himself written some rather Laforguian poems). For a young American to meet Laforgue by accident, part of the delight must have been that he was a surprise, off the beaten track, neither English nor canonical French. And his own conception of the history of poetry would change in order to give such a writer a new historical importance. The younger Eliot was very willing to rewrite history in this way.

He was, to the pleasure of some and the irritation of others, an allusive and acquisitive poet. In an essay on the Jacobean dramatist Philip Massinger (1920) he observed that "one of the surest of tests is the way in which a poet bor-

rows. Immature poets imitate, mature poets steal: bad poets
deface what they take, and good poets make it into some-
thing better, or at least something different."[13] His own no-
torious "stealing" is somewhat in the manner of the most
classical of the Jacobeans, Ben Jonson, who thought it right
"to convert the substance, or riches, of another poet, to his
own use"; and scholars have shown that even when Jonson
sounds most original he is actually stealing from someone
else. As Ian Donaldson remarks, "He perceived in the writers
of the past (as one might say) 'a part of himself,' or of the
self he sought assiduously to fashion."[14] Laforgue was only
one of the writers who, for Eliot, became "part of himself,"
and therefore available to be stolen from or adapted to what-
ever his private purpose was at the moment.

   One can read the Jacobean playwrights and the "meta-
physical" poets oneself and see what Eliot admired in them,
but to catch the flavor of Laforgue (1860–87) is not easy for
readers without French; indeed, it is probably most accessible
to Anglophones in the early work of Eliot himself. He had
acquired all three volumes of the French poet's works and
immersed himself in them, stealing from Laforgue in order
to produce not imitations but "something better, or at least
different." His study of the French poets of the nineteenth
century continued, and Laforgue led him to Corbière, Sté-
phane Mallarmé, and Charles Baudelaire. The transformation
of this essentially fin de siècle archive was Eliot's personal
achievement, and he shares with W. B. Yeats the credit for
having modernized the inheritance of that epoch. For a
while he even wrote in French—his four French poems are
here reprinted—and for a short time thought of continuing
to do so; and he always had a strong interest in France. His
student days in Paris had been fruitful, and they were illu-
minated by his love for Jean Verdenal, poet and medical
man, the dedicatee of his first book.

Among his other Parisian acquisitions was an admiration for Wagner, at one time very strong. Wagner was a great hero of the Symbolist poets, having united, as in their own way they hoped to do, the arts of music and poetry. Baudelaire had written a celebrated article in which he praised the composer for leaving a gap to be filled in by the listener's imagination—very much a part of Eliot's own program— *+ yeats* and for connecting modernity with myth—an achievement common to Wagner and James Joyce in *Ulysses*, a book Eliot, with one eye on his own program, warmly praised. The Wagnerian connection in *The Waste Land* is advertised by quotations from *Tristan und Isolde* and *The Ring*, and the allusion to *Parsifal*.[15] Eliot's enthusiasm for Wagner seems to have waned, but in these early days the composer was very much a part of that nineteenth-century inheritance—an inheritance by which Eliot set so much store that in his Clark lectures of 1926[16] he was willing to associate the French poets of that period with the best examples he could find in literary history, notably Dante and Donne (though his keenness on Donne was also fading).

So much for intellectual sources—and of course much more could be said of them. What of the poems themselves, and their extraordinary success in the world, their elevation to the vanguard of Modernism in poetry? At first they made their way quite modestly. Eliot was twenty-nine when, in 1917, his first book, *Prufrock and Other Observations*, appeared, forty pages long and priced at a shilling. (By the time the edition of five hundred copies was sold out it was 1921 and the price had gone up to five shillings.) In 1919 Leonard and Virginia Woolf printed *Poems by T. S. Eliot*, and in 1920 a small press issued *Ara Vos Prec*, reprinted in New York by Alfred A. Knopf as *Poems*, with slight alterations of order. All the early work Eliot approved of was now in print, except for *The Waste Land*, which followed in 1922. Meanwhile his admired essay collection *The Sacred Wood* (1920) had brought his name to the attention of a somewhat larger public. But these poems also had their admirers, and these readers were ready for the even more ambitious long poem that was to follow.

What had struck these admirers was the *newness* of the poems. They might have seen a connection with Browning's dramatic monologues, but the resemblance is not very close, as anybody can see by comparing "Gerontion" with, say, "Andrea del Sarto." And they would have seen the connection with French poetry of the period he admired. But Eliot's poems were unusual and new; they had no very unequivocal ancestry, and lacked any conventional consistency of style or setting. "Gerontion" opens with an unacknowledged allusion to a letter of Edward Fitzgerald's, breaks off from the account of a dismal domestic scene (also from Fitzgerald) to quote the New Testament and Bishop Lancelot Andrewes, before cutting to a passage borrowed from the autobiography of Henry Adams and some references, unexplained by the context, to three people whose names seem to be randomly assigned. There follows a tremendous pastiche of Jacobean dramatic verse; and so it continues, never less than surprising and unexpected. There is no followable story of the sort Browning provides, and Eliot has by now almost grown out of Laforguian allusive ironies. "Gerontion," which Eliot meant to place at the head of *The Waste Land* until Pound dissuaded him, is, like its successor, abnormal in lacking any certain perspective, even in the variety of its verse forms, which vary from free verse to mostly irregular iambic pentameters. (There was an intention to avoid the almost unavoidable English pentameter—one of Pound's marginalia in the manuscript of *The Waste Land* censures a line as being "too penty.")[17] The lack of conventional sequence, the abrupt and apparently irrational transitions, give the poem a private, dreamlike quality; there is a mood that is sustained, but no sequence, rather the random shifts of theme and image one experiences in dreams. And it might be said that the poet who wrote thus has already begun to create the taste by which he is relished.

The work of preparation was done in "Prufrock," "Portrait of a Lady," "Preludes," and "Rhapsody on a Windy Night." "Prufrock" already has that lack of waking definition, that unexpectedness and variety, though in a more domesticated, more self-ironical form. The exact social circumstances of Prufrock's "visit" are not explained. The poem lacks the severity and self-assurance of "Gerontion," and the figure of the fog strikes me as overdeveloped, a conceit prolonged too far. But "Prufrock" is for all that very bold, a triumph of innovation, as in the sudden incursion of the lines on the women and Michelangelo, the sudden reaching out from coffee spoons and polite chatter to comically large questions. We are transported from Prufrock's personal appearance to his hopeless aspirations: could he dare disturb the universe, could he hope to squeeze it into a ball, or achieve resurrection, or be spoken to by mermaids. One can imagine a story by Henry James that dealt, elusively of course, with a character like Prufrock, but hardly with *this* degree of elusiveness.

This was the poem by which Pound first recognized Eliot's gift, and he was probably interested less in its allusions than in its rhythmical variety, its power to confound the reader by saying, in reply to whatever questions he or she asks, "That is not what I meant at all," and say it so that the whole idea of Prufrock is expressed in wavering rhythms, so expressed that it retains an appropriate, beautiful indefiniteness even when the properties employed—trouser cuffs, haircuts, and so forth—are definite in themselves. "Portrait of a Lady," which has of course a Jamesian title, shares some of these characteristics: "I must borrow every changing shape / To find expression . . ." "Preludes" and "Rhapsody" are sketches of a mostly French urban waste land, and "La Figlia Che Piange" commemorates, with delicacy and variety, a mood, perhaps a scene, that will be centrally recalled in *The Waste Land*.

The quatrain poems are an exploration of a different path. "It may be that for some periods of society a more relaxed form of writing is right, and for others a more concentrated."[18] These poems are extremely concentrated, as if the intention was to find out if this was what "the age demanded."[19] But concentration aids rather than suppresses the habit of allusion. "Burbank with a Baedeker: Bleistein with a Cigar" has an epigraph—Eliot was fond of epigraphs—consisting of a whole string of unattributed quotations.

It is in these poems that we first meet the important figure of Sweeney, a dissolute bruiser who so fascinated Eliot that he was to make him the protagonist of that extraordinary but aborted dramatic experiment, *Sweeney Agonistes*. So it could be said that all the earlier poems can be seen by hindsight to look forward; but they should not be regarded merely as preparations for *The Waste Land* (and *Sweeney Agonistes*), for they are remarkable in themselves, and were seen by good judges to be so. Of course it remains true that they did prepare the way for the success of the great poem.

Some of that success was undoubtedly due also to the devoted support of Pound and of the New York lawyer John Quinn, whose generosity to artists was beyond praise. He worked with expert zeal in Eliot's interest, and was eventually rewarded by the poet's gift of the *Waste Land* manuscripts, which disappeared after his death and turned up only after Eliot's. The poet had thought them lost, and regretted the loss only because he would have liked them to survive as a record of Pound's work on the poem. It has been pointed out that before the publication of *The Waste Land* was negotiated with the small-circulation journal *The Dial* it was offered to *Vanity Fair*, a very different kind of magazine, witty and modish, to which Quinn was a contributor. Would the event of publication have seemed so portentous, the importance of the poem in relation to its world so sure, if that submission had succeeded?[20] However that may be, Eliot's admirers were quite exceptionally anxious to have the revised poem published, and to attract as much attention, and as much payment, for it as possible.

Eliot himself quite often spoke disparagingly of the poem that sealed his fame. "Various critics have done me the honour to interpret the poem in terms of criticism of the contemporary world, have considered it, indeed, an important piece of social criticism. To me it was only the relief of a personal and wholly insignificant grouse against life: it is just a piece of rhythmical grumbling."[21] And in 1931 he remarked that "when I wrote a poem called *The Waste Land* some of the more approving critics said that I had expressed the 'disillusionment of a generation,' which is nonsense. I may have expressed for them their own illusion of being disillusioned, but that did not form part of my intention."[22] (Here he seems to have forgotten his own repeated dictum, that the reader has the same interpretative rights as the author.) Toward the end of his life he took an even more censorious view: "I think that in the early poems it was a question . . . of not being able to—having more to say than one knew how to say, and having something one wanted to put into words and rhythm which one didn't have the command of words and rhythm to put in a way immediately apprehensible. That type of obscurity comes when a poet is still at the stage of learning how to use language. You have to say the thing the difficult way. The only alternative is not saying it at all, at that stage. . . . In *The Waste Land* I wasn't even bothering whether I understood what I was saying."[23]

Yet the poem surely belongs in spirit to the immediate postwar mood, and to the months when the poet was working through his breakdown: desolation within and without. Eliot must have been thinking about his own experience of illness while working on *The Waste Land*; as he once observed, "I know . . . that some forms of ill-health, debility or anaemia, may (if other circumstances are favourable) produce an efflux of poetry in a way approaching the condition of automatic writing"—a reference to his own experience during the composition of the last section of *The Waste Land*. And in a note to the passage just quoted he endorsed A. E. Housman's remark, "I have seldom written poetry unless I was rather out of health."[24] Moreover, it is clear that he himself originally attached great importance to this work. "It is, I think, much the best poem I have ever written," he claimed in a letter to a possible publisher, "and I think it would make a much more distinct impression and attract much more attention if published as a book."[25] *The Waste Land* must have been intended as part of the "effort to explore the frontiers of spirit [and] to regain, under very different conditions, what was known to men writing at remote times and in alien languages."[26] And this must be the case even though it is true that he wanted, when it was done, to put the poem behind him.[27]

The emphasis on book publication, which was eventually responsible for the addition of Eliot's notes, implies that the poet regarded the work as a single integral poem, though some early discussion of it treated it as a sequence of relatively discrete lyrics. The view that this is really the truth of the matter sometimes crops up in later criticism, especially when it is argued that Pound and Eliot interfered with the true course of *English* poetry, belonging as they did to a native American tradition, "the tradition of the new," which English poetry lacked.[28] No doubt it is conceivable that we have been induced by a sort of benign propaganda to see the poem as a single whole; but even if that is so, we have now agreed to see it thus, and we do see it thus. Eliot's explanation of our dubiety is different. He spoke of a "logic of the imagination" as opposed to "a logic of concepts": "People who do not appreciate poetry always find it difficult to distinguish between order and chaos in the arrangement of images."[29] The arrangement of images in *The Waste Land* (we came to agree) obeys the logic of the imagination. Eliot had found what Milton called "answerable style"— necessarily something new, for, as he expressed it many years later in *Little Gidding*,

> Last year's fruit is eaten,
> And the fullfed beast shall kick the empty pail.
> For last year's words belong to last year's language
> And next year's words await another voice.

The answerable style of *The Waste Land* had something in common with Cubism, which had revolutionized painting a few years earlier, and with the twelve-tone music invented by Arnold Schoenberg in place of the traditional scales; it permitted a view of history as without perspective, and a mode of composition that did not forget the past but perceived its methods as effects of mere custom rather than law, which the artist must now, as it were, get behind. And as Wordsworth, citing Coleridge, remarked, "every great and original writer, in proportion as he is great and original, must himself create the taste by which he is to be relished . . ."[30]

Here the question arises as to the seriousness of the claim that the poem has, after all, a binding deep structure, pro-

vided by Jessie Weston's book and the anthropological spec-
ulations of Sir James Frazer. It was Eliot himself, in one of
the notes he later deplored, who started the critics on a quest
for what might be called an anthropological foundation of
the poem. The work of the Cambridge school of anthro-
pologists, especially *The Golden Bough*, was fashionable at the
time, and there is no doubt that it interested Eliot. "Few
books are more fascinating than those of Miss [Jane] Har-
rison, Mr. [F. M.] Cornford, or Mr. [A. B.] Cook, when
they burrow in the origins of Greek myths and rites."[31]
Eliot's *The Sacred Wood* takes its title from Frazer's opening
pages, describing the slaying of the priest by his successor in
the sacred grove at Nemi.[32]

That a deep mythical structure would have satisfied one
of Eliot's aspirations is suggested by his praise of Joyce's *Ulys-
ses* (1922), part of a publicity campaign on behalf of another
great and original book. Referring to Joyce's "parallel use of
The Odyssey," he maintains that "[i]n using the myth, in
manipulating a continuous parallel between contemporaneity
and antiquity, Mr. Joyce is pursuing a method which others
must pursue after him. . . . It is simply a way of controlling,
of ordering, of giving a shape and a significance to the im-
mense panorama of futility and anarchy which is contem-
porary history."[33] The question remains whether Eliot's use
of his myth is quite as systematic as Joyce's. That it probably
isn't is suggested by the genesis of the poem; in the drafts
there was much material which could not readily be assim-
ilated to the myth. But this does not mean that the allusions
to Frazer and Weston are entirely frivolous; these writers did
supply some of the plan "and a good deal of the incidental
symbolism of the poem," as Eliot says in his opening note.
Perhaps we should not look for anything too cut-and-dried;
the poet had surrendered to so much—to Laforgue, to
Baudelaire, to Dante, to Webster, to Donne, to Henry

James, to Bradley, to Wagner—that an undefinable mass of material blended with a current interest in Frazerian mythography, and Weston's aligning of the old myths and rites with the Grail legends.

Another aspect one should not overlook is the poem's powerful atmosphere of impending apocalypse. Parallels with Virgil's *Aeneid* have often, and justly, been proposed, for that poem is about the death of a civilization and is full of burning, collapsing cities.[34] Eliot's poem is a city poem, a London poem; the city which inherited the imperium of Rome, the eternal city, lies waste. The biblical apocalypse and its Babylon are also in the shadows of the poem:

> [T]he merchants of the earth are waxed rich. . . . And the kings of the earth, who have committed fornication and live deliciously with her, shall bewail her, and lament for her, when they shall see the smoke of her burning. . . . And every shipmaster, and the company of ships, and sailors, and as many as trade by the sea, stood afar off, and cried when they saw the smoke of her burning, saying, What city is like unto this great city! (Rev. 18:3, 9–18)

The Waste Land is probably Eliot's most striking achievement, though he never ceased from exploration, and all his subsequent poetry has a deeply considered originality. At the time of writing *The Waste Land* he is said to have remarked that he was closer to being a Buddhist than anything else. The religious education of his youth had been Unitarian, but with his strong idea of tradition he became closer to one form of Catholic Christianity, and in 1928 was baptized and confirmed in the Church of England. Meanwhile his poetry took on a Christian tone, especially in *Ash-Wednesday* (published 1930) and in his final work, *Four Quartets* (written 1936–41 and published together in 1943). He had, over this period, continued to interest himself in verse drama, though, characteristically, his later attempts did not at all resemble *Sweeney Agonistes*. *Murder in the Cathedral* (1935), a play about the martyrdom of Thomas à Becket, was performed in Canterbury cathedral and elsewhere with considerable success; it experiments with a chorus, and has many fine passages, though the poet himself regarded it as a dead end, and wrote *The Family Reunion* (1939) for the secular theater, inventing a form of verse which could carry quite commonplace as well as exalted choric dialogue. *The Cocktail Party* (1950) was probably the most successful of his plays. Even in works intended for the commercial theater he showed a continuing interest in the relation between the new and the old, for Euripides' *Alcestis* lurks behind *The Cocktail Party*, and his *Ion* behind *The Confidential Clerk* (1953).

Despite his measure of theatrical success and his extraordinary general fame, he cannot be said to have brought off the feat of restoring verse to the theater—an effort in which many others, including W. H. Auden, Ronald Duncan, and Christopher Fry also failed. The same neglect seems to have befallen his social criticism, for it is rarely invoked even on the extreme political right.

These are relatively unimportant failures. Eliot's true distinction is as a poet, and the early poems establish what the later poems confirm: taken together, they constitute a strong claim for Eliot's primacy among twentieth-century poets in English.

NOTES TO THE INTRODUCTION

1. Hugh Kenner, *The Invisible Poet* (1959), p. 38.

2. In a review in *The Criterion* vol. ix (January 1930).

3. Quoted by Donald Gallup, "T. S. Eliot & Ezra Pound: Collaborators in Letters," *The Atlantic Monthly*, January 1970.

4. Letter to Harriet Monroe (editor of *Poetry*) 22 September 1914, in D. D. Paige, ed., *Ezra Pound: Selected Letters, 1907–1941* (1950), p. 40.

5. In an interview with Donald Hall in *Paris Review,* vol. 21, 1959. Reprinted in Donald Hall, ed., *Remembering Poets: Reminiscences and Opinions* (1978). A good account of the Eliot-Pound relationship is Gallup, "T. S. Eliot & Ezra Pound." See also Timothy Materer, *Vortex: Pound, Eliot, and Lewis* (1979) and Erik Svarny, *"The Men of 1914": T. S. Eliot and Early Modernism* (1988).

6. See Eliot's essays "The Metaphysical Poets" and "Andrew Marvell" in *Selected Essays* (1932, and many later editions); and *The Varieties of Metaphysical Poetry*, ed. R. Schuchard (1993). This consists of lectures given at Cambridge in 1926, and brings together most of Eliot's views on seventeenth-century English poetry, his favorite French poets, and Dante.

7. Stephen Spender, "Remembering Eliot," in Allen Tate, ed., *T. S. Eliot: The Man and His Work* (1966), pp. 55–6.

8. *Selected Essays*, pp. 17–22.

9. *Selected Essays*, p. 20.

10. Roland Barthes, *The Pleasure of the Text*, trans. Richard Miller (1976).

11. *Selected Essays*, pp. 250, 273.

12. "Ezra Pound," *Poetry*, September 1956, p. 330. Grover Smith has pointed out that this remark is imprecise. Pound saw the manuscript in 1921, and what he saw was "an aggregation of drafts" that could still be thought of as a series of poems rather than as one poem. And Eliot kept control of the work; out of gratitude he may have rather exaggerated Pound's contribution, which was nevertheless of great importance. Grover Smith, "The Making of *The Waste Land*," *Mosaic* (fall 1972), pp. 127–8.

13. *Selected Essays*, p. 206.

14. Ian Donaldson, *Jonson's Magic Houses* (1997), p. 39.

15. It may also be important that he had been impressed by Stravinsky's *Sacre du printemps*, a work which caused a riot at its first Paris performance in 1913. Stravinsky's ballet is about a primitive spring ritual, but the music was very modern; Eliot said it evoked "the scream of the motor horn, the rattle of machinery, the grind of wheels, the beating of iron and steel, the roar of the underground railway, and other barbaric cries of modern life." (Quoted in Monroe Spears, *Dionysus in the City* [1970] p. 80.)

16. Now belatedly published: see note 6 above.

17. Valerie Eliot, ed., *The Waste Land: A Facsimile and Transcript of the Original Drafts, Including the Annotations of Ezra Pound* (1971), p. 11. The line is now 101 of the poem; Eliot as it happens, retained it without change.

18. *The Use of Poetry and the Use of Criticism* (1933), pp. 152–3.

19. See Pound's "Hugh Selwyn Mauberley," which also explores the French-style quatrain, and was, like these poems of Eliot's, written as a deliberate attempt to avoid the "slushiness" of contemporary British verse.

20. For an excellent account of the prehistory of publication see Lawrence Rainey, "The Price of Modernism: Publishing *The Waste Land*" in Ronald Bush, ed., *T. S. Eliot: The Modernist in History* (1991), pp. 91–133. Rainey emphasizes the commercial aspect of Eliot's dealing with publishers, and reckons that the poet made about $2,800 from the poem, equivalent in 1991 terms to about $45,000–$55,000. Rainey remarks that some of this money was provided by people who had not read the poem. See also Daniel H. Woodward, "Notes on the Publishing History and Text of *The Waste Land*," in C. B. Cox and Arnold Hinchliffe, eds., *T. S. Eliot: The Waste Land* (1968), pp. 71–90.

21. Remark reported by Theodore Spencer and recorded by the poet's brother, Henry Ware Eliot. It is printed as an epigraph in Valerie Eliot's edition of the manuscripts.

22. "Thoughts After Lambeth," in *Selected Essays*, p. 324.

23. Interview in *Writers at Work: The Paris Review Interviews* (1965), pp. 104–5, quoted by Helen Gardner, *The Composition of "Four Quartets"* (1978), p. 4.

24. *The Use of Poetry and the Use of Criticism* (1933), p. 144–5. And see Valerie Eliot, ed., *T. S. Eliot: The Waste Land* (1971), note on "What the Thunder said," p. 129.

25. Letter to Maurice Firuski in the Chapin Library, Williams College (copyright of Valerie Eliot), quoted in Rainey (see note 20).

26. *Selected Essays,* p. 274.

27. See Valerie Eliot, ed., *T. S. Eliot: The Waste Land*, p. xxv.

28. For the most persuasive of such arguments see Graham Hough, *Image and Experience* (1960). One example: Hough stresses the fortuity of Phlebas's appearance in the poem—he had a previous existence elsewhere, and is got in only by some arbitrary preparation in the lines about Madame Sosostris.

29. Foreword to Eliot's translation of Saint-John Perse, *Anabasis* (1930).

30. Letter to Lady Beaumont, 21 May 1807, in Alan G. Hill, ed., *Selected Letters of William Wordsworth* (1984), p. 103.

31. T. S. Eliot, *The Sacred Wood* (1920), pp. 75–6. The authors mentioned are all associated with the Cambridge school and Frazer.

32. For a full account of the thesis that Frazer influenced both the structure and the incidentals of the poem, see John B. Vickery, *The Literary Impact of "The Golden Bough"* (1973), pp. 233–79.

33. "*Ulysses*, Order and Myth," *The Dial*, November 1923; reprinted in F. Kermode, ed., *Selected Prose of T. S. Eliot* (1975), pp. 175–8.

34. See Hugh Kenner, "The Urban Apocalypse," in A. Walton Litz, ed., *Eliot in His Time* (1973), pp. 23–49; Gareth Reeves, "*The Waste Land* and the *Aeneid*," *Modern Language Review*, July 1987, pp. 555–72; and Charles Martindale, "Ruins of Rome: T. S. Eliot and the Presence of the Past," *Arion*, fall/winter 1995/6, pp. 102–140.

SUGGESTIONS FOR FURTHER READING

The volume of criticism and commentary on these poems is so huge that any list as this must be selective and somewhat arbitrary. Some studies in periodicals and some longer specialist works not included here are mentioned in the notes to the introduction.

The standard bibliography is Donald Gallup's *T. S. Eliot: A Bibliography* (1952 and later editions).

Of Eliot's own prose works, his first critical book, *The Sacred Wood* (1920), is most relevant for the period of these poems, but later collections often contain illuminating observations: *Selected Essays* (1932), *The Use of Poetry and the Use of Criticism* (1933), *After Strange Gods* (1934), *Essays Ancient and Modern* (1936), *On Poetry and Poets* (1957), *To Criticize the Critic* (1965). For poems earlier than those included here see Christopher Ricks, *Inventions of the March Hare: Poems 1909–1917* (1996). All Eliot's books except *After Strange Gods* have been reprinted often.

Some manuscript versions of the poems here reprinted are included in Ricks's edition. Readers of *The Waste Land* should probably take the poet's advice and read Jessie L. Weston's *From Ritual to Romance* (1920) and James Frazer's *The Golden Bough*, of which there is an abridged edition (1922 and later reprintings). On Frazer's influence see John B. Vickery, *The Literary Impact of "The Golden Bough"* (1973), especially chapter 7.

For biography, see Valerie Eliot's *The Letters of T. S. Eliot*, vol. 1 (1988), and Lyndall Gordon, *Eliot's Early Years* (1978) and *Eliot's New Life* (1988). A valuable earlier contribution is Herbet Howarth, *Notes on Some Figures Behind T. S. Eliot* (1964). Bernard Bergonzi's *T. S. Eliot* (1972) is a good critical biography. On accusations of anti-Semitism, see Christopher Ricks, *T. S. Eliot and Prejudice* (1988) and Anthony Julius, *T. S. Eliot: Anti-Semitism and Literary Form* (1995). These books also offer valuable critical and interpretative comments. On Eliot's politics more generally see W. M. Chace, *The Political Identities of Ezra Pound and T. S. Eliot* (1973); Roger Kojecky, *T. S. Eliot's Social Criticism* (1971); and Paul Morrison, *The Poetics of Fascism* (1996).

A selection of criticism over a long period can be found in Michael Grant, ed., *T. S. Eliot: The Critical Heritage*, 2 vols. (1982). The following list includes some of the more important early books on Eliot, and some more recent book-length studies.

F. O. Matthiessen, *The Achievement of T. S. Eliot*, 3rd ed. (1959).

Hugh Kenner, *The Invisible Poet* (1959).

C. K. Stead, *The New Poetic* (1964) and *Pound, Yeats, Eliot and the Modernist Movement* (1986), which has good comments on the earlier poems, and an appendix on the dating and drafts of *The Waste Land*.

Eric Thompson, *T. S. Eliot: The Man and his Works* (1969).

Stephen Spender, *T. S. Eliot* (1975). Spender had written on Eliot much earlier, in *The Destructive Element* (1938). He had the advantage of close personal friendship with Eliot.

A. D. Moody, *Thomas Stearns Eliot, Poet* (1979).

Ronald Bush, *T. S. Eliot: A Study in Character and Style* (1983).

Robert Crawford, *The Savage and the City in the Work of T. S. Eliot* (1987).

Stanley Sultan, *Eliot, Joyce and Company* (1987).

Eric Svarny, *"The Men of 1914": T. S. Eliot and Early Modernism* (1988).

Jewel Spears Brooker and Joseph Bentley, *Reading the Waste Land* (1990).

There are some good collections of essays:

Richard Marsh and Tambimutti, eds., *T. S. Eliot* (1948). Celebrates the poet's sixtieth birthday with essays by many of his friends and associates.

B. Rajan, *T. S. Eliot: A Study of His Writings by Several Hands* (1948). Includes Cleanth Brooks on *The Waste Land*.

Allen Tate, ed., *T. S. Eliot: The Man and his Work* (1967). Memorial volume; memoirs by Herbert Read, Stephen Spender, and Ezra Pound, as well as several critical essays.

Graham Martin, ed., *Eliot in Perspective* (1970).

A. Walton Litz, ed., *Eliot in His Time* (1973). On the fiftieth anniversary of *The Waste Land*: essays by such scholars as Hugh Kenner, Helen Gardner, Robert M. Adams, Donald Davie.

Ronald Bush, ed., *T. S. Eliot: The Modernist in History* (1991).

These are valuable commentaries:

Grover Smith, *T. S. Eliot's Poetry and Plays: A Study in Sources and Meaning* (1956).

Brian Southam, *A Student's Guide to the Selected Poems of T. S. Eliot*, 6th ed. (1994).

The present editor acknowledges much indebtedness to these commentators.

1888   Born in St. Louis, Missouri, 26 September.

1906   Freshman at Harvard.

1910   Graduated, having published verse in *The Harvard Advocate* and served on its editorial board. In October went to France, attended the philosophical lectures of Henri Bergson, and became a friend of Jean Verdenal, whose death in action in 1915 is commemorated in the dedication of *Prufrock and Other Observations*.

1911   Visited London, Munich, and Italy. Returned to Harvard to work for his doctorate. Final version of "Prufrock" and "Portrait of a Lady."

1912   Taught philosophy as an assistant at Harvard.

1913   Read F. H. Bradley's *Appearance and Reality*.

1914   Met Bertrand Russell in Cambridge, Massachusetts (March) and Ezra Pound in London (September). Continued study of Bradley at Merton College, Oxford.

1915   Jean Verdenal killed at the Dardanelles, 2 May. Eliot married Vivian Haigh-Wood, 26 June. "Prufrock," "Preludes," "Rhapsody," "Portrait of a Lady," "The Boston Evening Transcript," "Aunt Helen," and "Cousin Nancy" published in periodicals. Spent summer in United States, decided thenceforth to live in England, returned there in August and became a schoolteacher.

1916   Submitted thesis to Harvard, where it was approved, but Eliot never completed the formalities by attending an oral examination. Lectured on

French and English literature and wrote reviews, some in technical philosophical journals.

1917   Began work in Lloyd's Bank in the City of London. *Prufrock and Other Observations* published by *The Egoist*. Appointed assistant editor of *The Egoist*. Augmented income by lecturing.

1919   *Poems* published by Hogarth Press. Invited to write leading articles for *Times Literary Supplement*.

1920   *Ara Vos Prec* published in London, and a little later, with changes in the order of the poems, issued as *Poems* in New York. Working on *The Waste Land*. Published *The Sacred Wood*, a collection of literary criticism.

1921   *The Waste Land* in progress. With Lady Rothermere's sponsorship Eliot planned a new review, *The Criterion*. His health having broken down, he obtained leave from bank and took a rest cure, first at Margate and then in Lausanne, Switzerland. In November visited Pound in Paris and handed him the drafts of *The Waste Land*.

1922   Ill and in financial difficulties. Friends tried to get up a fund to help. *The Dial* prize award of $2,000. In October *The Waste Land* published, without notes, in the first issue of *The Criterion* and in *The Dial*. In December *The Waste Land* published as a book by Boni & Liveright, New York, with the addition of the explanatory notes.

THE WASTE LAND
AND OTHER POEMS

PRUFROCK

AND OTHER OBSERVATIONS

1917

For Jean Verdenal, 1889–1915
mort aux Dardanelles[1]

Or puoi la quantitate
comprender dell'amor ch'a te mi scalda,
quando dismento nostra vanitate,
trattando l'ombre come cosa salda.[2]

THE LOVE SONG OF
J. ALFRED PRUFROCK

S'io credessi che mia risposta fosse
a persona che mai tornasse al mondo,
questa fiamma staria senza più scosse.
Ma perciocchè che giammai di questo fondo
non tornò vivo alcun, s'i'odo il vero,
senza tema d'infamia ti rispondo.[1]

Let us go then, you and I,
When the evening is spread out against the sky
Like a patient etherised[2] upon a table;
Let us go, through certain half-deserted streets,
The muttering retreats
Of restless nights in one-night cheap hotels
And sawdust restaurants with oyster-shells:
Streets that follow like a tedious argument
Of insidious intent
To lead you to an overwhelming question . . .
Oh, do not ask, "What is it?"
Let us go and make our visit.

In the room the women come and go
Talking of Michelangelo.[3]

The yellow fog that rubs its back upon the window-
panes,
The yellow smoke that rubs its muzzle on the
window-panes,

Licked its tongue into the corners of the evening,
Lingered upon the pools that stand in drains,
Let fall upon its back the soot that falls from
      chimneys,
20   Slipped by the terrace, made a sudden leap,
And seeing that it was a soft October night,
Curled once about the house, and fell asleep.

And indeed there will be time[4]
For the yellow smoke that slides along the street
25   Rubbing its back upon the window-panes;
There will be time, there will be time
To prepare a face to meet the faces that you meet;
There will be time to murder and create,
And time for all the works and days of hands
30   That lift and drop a question on your plate;
Time for you and time for me,
And time yet for a hundred indecisions,
And for a hundred visions and revisions,
Before the taking of a toast and tea.

35   In the room the women come and go
Talking of Michelangelo.

And indeed there will be time
To wonder, "Do I dare?" and, "Do I dare?"
Time to turn back and descend the stair,
40   With a bald spot in the middle of my hair—
(They will say: "How his hair is growing thin!")
My morning coat, my collar mounting firmly to the
      chin,
My necktie rich and modest, but asserted by a simple
      pin—
(They will say: "But how his arms and legs are
      thin!")

45   Do I dare
Disturb the universe?
In a minute there is time
For decisions and revisions which a minute will
    reverse.

For I have known them all already, known them
    all—
50   Have known the evenings, mornings, afternoons,
I have measured out my life with coffee spoons;
I know the voices dying with a dying fall[5]
Beneath the music from a farther room.
    So how should I presume?

55   And I have known the eyes already, known them
    all—
The eyes that fix you in a formulated phrase,
And when I am formulated, sprawling on a pin,
When I am pinned and wriggling on the wall,
Then how should I begin
60   To spit out all the butt-ends of my days and ways?
    And how should I presume?
And I have known the arms already, known them
    all—
Arms that are braceleted and white and bare
(But in the lamplight, downed with light brown
    hair!)
65   Is it perfume from a dress[6]
That makes me so digress?
Arms that lie along a table, or wrap about a shawl.
    And should I then presume?
    And how should I begin?

      .   .   .   .

70   Shall I say, I have gone at dusk through narrow
    streets

And watched the smoke that rises from the pipes
Of lonely men in shirt-sleeves, leaning out of
    windows? . . .
    I should have been a pair of ragged claws
Scuttling across the floors of silent seas.

                    ·   ·   ·   ·

75   And the afternoon, the evening, sleeps so peacefully!
Smoothed by long fingers,
Asleep . . . tired . . . or it malingers,
Stretched on the floor, here beside you and me.
Should I, after tea and cakes and ices,
80   Have the strength to force the moment to its crisis?
But though I have wept and fasted, wept and prayed,
Though I have seen my head (grown slightly bald)
    brought in upon a platter,[7]
I am no prophet—and here's no great matter;
I have seen the moment of my greatness flicker,
And I have seen the eternal Footman hold my coat,
85   and snicker,
And in short, I was afraid.

And would it have been worth it, after all,
After the cups, the marmalade, the tea,
Among the porcelain, among some talk of you and
    me,
90   Would it have been worth while,
To have bitten off the matter with a smile,
To have squeezed the universe into a ball[8]
To roll it towards some overwhelming question,
To say: "I am Lazarus,[9] come from the dead,
95   Come back to tell you all, I shall tell you all"—
If one, settling a pillow by her head,
    Should say: "That is not what I meant at all.
    That is not it, at all."

And would it have been worth it, after all,
100   Would it have been worth while,
After the sunsets and the dooryards and the sprinkled
    streets,
After the novels, after the teacups, after the skirts that
    trail along the floor—
And this, and so much more?—
It is impossible to say just what I mean!
105   But as if a magic lantern threw the nerves in patterns
    on a screen:
Would it have been worth while
If one, settling a pillow by her head,
Should say, "That is not what I meant at all;
    "That is not it, at all."

.   .   .

110   No! I am not Prince Hamlet, nor was meant to be;
Am an attendant lord, one that will do
To swell a progress,[10] start a scene or two,
Advise the prince; no doubt,[11] an easy tool,
Deferential, glad to be of use,
115   Politic,[12] cautious, and meticulous;
Full of high sentence,[13] but a bit obtuse;
At times, indeed, almost ridiculous—
Almost, at times, the Fool.[14]

I grow old . . . I grow old . . .
120   I shall wear the bottoms of my trousers rolled.[15]

Shall I part my hair behind?[16] Do I dare to eat a
    peach?
I shall wear white flannel trousers, and walk upon the
    beach.
I have heard the mermaids singing,[17] each to each.

I do not think that they will sing to me.

125   I have seen them riding seaward on the waves
Combing the white hair of the waves blown back
When the wind blows the water white and black.

We have lingered in the chambers of the sea
By sea-girls wreathed with seaweed red and brown
130   Till human voices wake us, and we drown.

PORTRAIT OF A LADY

Thou hast committed—
Fornication: but that was in another country,
And besides, the wench is dead.[1]
THE JEW OF MALTA

I

Among the smoke and fog of a December
afternoon
You have the scene arrange itself—as it will seem to
do—
With "I have saved this afternoon for you";
And four wax candles in the darkened room,
Four rings of light upon the ceiling overhead,
An atmosphere of Juliet's tomb
Prepared for all the things to be said, or left unsaid.
We have been, let us say, to hear the latest Pole
Transmit the Preludes,[2] through his hair and finger-
tips.
"So intimate, this Chopin, that I think his soul
Should be resurrected only among friends
Some two or three, who will not touch the bloom
That is rubbed and questioned in the concert room."
—And so the conversation slips
Among velleities and carefully caught regrets
Through attenuated tones of violins
Mingled with remote cornets
And begins.
"You do not know how much they mean to me, my
friends,

20 And how, how rare and strange it is, to find
In a life composed so much, so much of odds and
    ends,
(For indeed I do not love it . . . you knew? you are
    not blind!
How keen you are!)
To find a friend who has these qualities,
25 Who has, and gives
Those qualities upon which friendship lives.
How much it means that I say this to you—
Without these friendships—life, what *cauchemar!*"[3]

Among the windings of the violins
30 And the ariettes
Of cracked cornets
Inside my brain a dull tom-tom begins
Absurdly hammering a prelude of its own,
Capricious monotone
35 That is at least one definite "false note."
—Let us take the air, in a tobacco trance,
Admire the monuments,
Discuss the late events,
Correct our watches by the public clocks.
40 Then sit for half an hour and drink our bocks.

II

    Now that lilacs are in bloom
She has a bowl of lilacs in her room
And twists one in her fingers while she talks.
"Ah, my friend, you do not know, you do not know
45 What life is, you who hold it in your hands";
(Slowly twisting the lilac stalks)
"You let it flow from you, you let it flow,

And youth is cruel, and has no more remorse
And smiles at situations which it cannot see."
I smile, of course,
50   And go on drinking tea.
      "Yet with these April sunsets, that somehow recall
My buried life,[4] and Paris in the Spring,
I feel immeasurably at peace, and find the world
55   To be wonderful and youthful, after all."

The voice returns like the insistent out-of-tune
Of a broken violin on an August afternoon:
"I am always sure that you understand
My feelings, always sure that you feel,
60   Sure that across the gulf you reach your hand.

You are invulnerable, you have no Achilles' heel.
You will go on, and when you have prevailed
You can say: at this point many a one has failed.
But what have I, but what have I, my friend,
65   To give you, what can you receive from me?
Only the friendship and the sympathy
Of one about to reach her journey's end.

I shall sit here, serving tea to friends. . . ."

I take my hat: how can I make a cowardly amends
70   For what she has said to me?
You will see me any morning in the park
Reading the comics and the sporting page.
Particularly I remark
An English countess goes upon the stage.
75   A Greek was murdered at a Polish dance,
Another bank defaulter has confessed.
I keep my countenance,

I remain self-possessed
Except when a street-piano, mechanical and tired
80   Reiterates some worn-out common song
With the smell of hyacinths across the garden
Recalling things that other people have desired.
Are these ideas right or wrong?

III

The October night comes down: returning as
before
85   Except for a slight sensation of being ill at ease
I mount the stairs and turn the handle of the door
And feel as if I had mounted on my hands and
knees.
"And so you are going abroad; and when do you
return?
But that's a useless question.
90   You hardly know when you are coming back,
You will find so much to learn."
My smile falls heavily among the bric-à-brac.

"Perhaps you can write to me."
My self-possession flares up for a second;
95   *This* is as I had reckoned.
"I have been wondering frequently of late
(But our beginnings never know our ends!)
Why we have not developed into friends."
I feel like one who smiles, and turning shall remark
100 Suddenly, his expression in a glass.
My self-possession gutters; we are really in the dark.

"For everybody said so, all our friends,
They all were sure our feelings would relate

So closely! I myself can hardly understand.
105   We must leave it now to fate.
You will write, at any rate.
Perhaps it is not too late.
I shall sit here, serving tea to friends."

And I must borrow every changing shape
To find expression . . . dance, dance
110   Like a dancing bear,
Cry like a parrot, chatter like an ape.
Let us take the air, in a tobacco trance—

Well! and what if she should die some afternoon,
115   Afternoon grey and smoky, evening yellow and rose;
Should die and leave me sitting pen in hand
With the smoke coming down above the housetops;
Doubtful, for quite a while
Not knowing what to feel or if I understand
Or whether wise or foolish, tardy or too soon . . .
120   Would she not have the advantage, after all?
This music is successful with a "dying fall"
Now that we talk of dying—
And should I have the right to smile?

PRELUDES

I

The winter evening settles down
With smell of steaks in passageways.
Six o'clock.
The burnt-out ends of smoky days.
And now a gusty shower wraps
The grimy scraps
Of withered leaves about your feet
And newspapers from vacant lots;
The showers beat
On broken blinds and chimney-pots,
And at the corner of the street
A lonely cab-horse steams and stamps.
And then the lighting of the lamps.

II

The morning comes to consciousness
Of faint stale smells of beer
From the sawdust-trampled street
With all its muddy feet that press
To early coffee-stands.
With the other masquerades
That time resumes,
One thinks of all the hands
That are raising dingy shades
In a thousand furnished rooms.

III

You tossed a blanket from the bed,
You lay upon your back, and waited;
You dozed, and watched the night revealing
The thousand sordid images
5   Of which your soul was constituted;
They flickered against the ceiling.
And when all the world came back
And the light crept up between the shutters,
And you heard the sparrows in the gutters,
10   You had such a vision of the street
As the street hardly understands;
Sitting along the bed's edge, where
You curled the papers from your hair,
Or clasped the yellow soles of feet
15   In the palms of both soiled hands.

IV

His soul stretched tight across the skies
That fade behind a city block,
Or trampled by insistent feet
At four and five and six o'clock;
5   And short square fingers stuffing pipes,
And evening newspapers, and eyes
Assured of certain certainties,
The conscience of a blackened street
Impatient to assume the world.
10   I am moved by fancies that are curled
Around these images, and cling:
The notion of some infinitely gentle
Infinitely suffering thing.

Wipe your hand across your mouth, and laugh;
15   The worlds revolve like ancient women
    Gathering fuel in vacant lots.

RHAPSODY ON A WINDY NIGHT

Twelve o'clock.
Along the reaches of the street
Held in a lunar synthesis,
Whispering lunar incantations
5 Dissolve the floors of the memory
And all its clear relations,
Its divisions and precisions.
Every street-lamp that I pass
Beats like a fatalistic drum,
10 And through the spaces of the dark
Midnight shakes the memory
As a madman shakes a dead geranium.[1]

Half-past one,
The street-lamp sputtered,
15 The street-lamp muttered,
The street-lamp said, "Regard[2] that woman
Who hesitates toward you in the light of the door
Which opens on her like a grin.
You see the border of her dress
20 Is torn and stained with sand,
And you see the corner of her eye
Twists like a crooked pin."

The memory throws up high and dry
A crowd of twisted things;
25 A twisted branch upon the beach
Eaten smooth, and polished
As if the world gave up
The secret of its skeleton,

Stiff and white.
30   A broken spring in a factory yard,
Rust that clings to the form that the strength has left
Hard and curled and ready to snap.

Half-past two,
The street-lamp said,
35   "Remark the cat which flattens itself in the gutter,
Slips out its tongue
And devours a morsel of rancid butter."
So the hand of the child, automatic,
Slipped out and pocketed a toy that was running
    along the quay.
40   I could see nothing behind that child's eye.[3]
I have seen eyes in the street
Trying to peer through lighted shutters,
And a crab one afternoon in a pool,
An old crab with barnacles on his back,
45   Gripped the end of a stick which I held him.

Half-past three,
The lamp sputtered,
The lamp muttered in the dark.
The lamp hummed:
50   "Regard the moon,
La lune ne garde aucune rancune,[4]
She winks a feeble eye,
She smiles into corners.
She smooths the hair of the grass.
55   The moon has lost her memory.
A washed-out smallpox cracks her face,
Her hand twists a paper rose,
That smells of dust and old Cologne,
She is alone

60 With all the old nocturnal smells
    That cross and cross across her brain.
    The reminiscence comes
    Of sunless dry geraniums
    And dust in crevices,
65 Smells of chestnuts in the streets,
    And female smells in shuttered rooms,[5]
    And cigarettes in corridors
    And cocktail smells in bars."

    The lamp said,
70 "Four o'clock,
    Here is the number on the door.
    Memory!
    You have the key,
    The little lamp spreads a ring on the stair.
75 Mount.
    The bed is open; the tooth-brush hangs on the wall,
    Put your shoes at the door,[6] sleep, prepare for life."

    The last twist of the knife.

MORNING AT THE WINDOW

They are rattling breakfast plates in basement kitchens,
And along the trampled edges of the street
I am aware of the damp souls of housemaids
Sprouting despondently at area gates.

5   The brown waves of fog toss up to me
Twisted faces from the bottom of the street,
And tear from a passer-by with muddy skirts
An aimless smile that hovers in the air
And vanishes along the level of the roofs.

The readers of the *Boston Evening Transcript*
Sway in the wind like a field of ripe corn.

When evening quickens faintly in the street,
Wakening the appetites of life in some
And to others bringing the *Boston Evening Transcript*,
I mount the steps and ring the bell, turning
Wearily, as one would turn to nod good-bye to La
    Rochefoucauld,[1]
If the street were time and he at the end of the street,
And I say, "Cousin Harriet, here is the *Boston Evening
    Transcript*."

AUNT HELEN

Miss Helen Slingsby was my maiden aunt,
And lived in a small house near a fashionable square
Cared for by servants to the number of four.
Now when she died there was silence in heaven[1]
And silence at her end of the street.
The shutters were drawn and the undertaker wiped
    his feet—
He was aware that this sort of thing had occurred
    before.
The dogs were handsomely provided for,
But shortly afterwards the parrot died too.
The Dresden clock[2] continued ticking on the
    mantelpiece,
And the footman sat upon the dining-table
Holding the second housemaid on his knees—
Who had always been so careful while her mistress
    lived.

COUSIN NANCY

Miss Nancy Ellicott
Strode across the hills and broke them,
Rode across the hills and broke them—
The barren New England hills—
Riding to hounds
Over the cow-pasture.

Miss Nancy Ellicott smoked
And danced all the modern dances;
And her aunts were not quite sure how they felt
    about it,
But they knew that it was modern.

Upon the glazen shelves kept watch
Matthew and Waldo,[1] guardians of the faith,
The army of unalterable law.[2]

MR. APOLLINAX

Ω τῆς καινότητος. Ἡράκλεις, τῆς παραδοξολογίας.
εὐμήχανος ἄνθρωπος.[1]

Lucian

When Mr. Apollinax visited the United States
His laughter tinkled among the teacups.
I thought of Fragilion,[2] that shy figure among the
    birch-trees,
And of Priapus[3] in the shrubbery
Gaping at the lady in the swing.
In the palace of Mrs. Phlaccus, at Professor Channing-
    Cheetah's
He laughed like an irresponsible foetus.
His laughter was submarine and profound
Like the old man of the sea's
Hidden under coral islands
Where worried bodies of drowned men drift down in
    the green silence,[4]
Dropping from fingers of surf.
I looked for the head of Mr. Apollinax rolling under a
    chair
Or grinning over a screen
With seaweed in its hair.
I heard the beat of centaur's hoofs over the hard turf
As his dry and passionate talk devoured the afternoon.
"He is a charming man"—"But after all what did he
    mean?"—

"His pointed ears. . . . He must be unbalanced."—

20   "There was something he said that I might have
    challenged."

Of dowager Mrs. Phlaccus, and Professor and Mrs.
  Cheetah

I remember a slice of lemon, and a bitten macaroon.

HYSTERIA

As she laughed I was aware of becoming involved in her laughter and being part of it, until her teeth were only accidental stars with a talent for squad-drill. I was drawn in by short gasps, inhaled at each momentary recovery, lost finally in the dark caverns of her throat, bruised by the ripple of unseen muscles. An elderly waiter with trembling hands was hurriedly spreading a pink and white checked cloth over the rusty green iron table, saying: "If the lady and gentleman wish to take their tea in the garden, if the lady and gentleman wish to take their tea in the garden . . ." I decided that if the shaking of her breasts could be stopped, some of the fragments of the afternoon might be collected, and I concentrated my attention with careful subtlety to this end.

CONVERSATION GALANTE

I observe: "Our sentimental friend the moon!
Or possibly (fantastic, I confess)
It may be Prester John's[1] balloon
Or an old battered lantern hung aloft
5   To light poor travellers to their distress."
        She then: "How you digress!"

And I then: "Someone frames upon the keys
That exquisite nocturne, with which we explain
The night and moonshine; music which we seize
10   To body forth our own vacuity."
        She then: "Does this refer to me?"
        "Oh no, it is I who am inane."

"You, madam, are the eternal humorist,
The eternal enemy of the absolute,
15   Giving our vagrant moods the slightest twist!
With your air indifferent and imperious
At a stroke our mad poetics to confute—"
        And—"Are we then so serious?"

LA FIGLIA CHE PIANGE[1]

O quam te memorem virgo . . .[2]

Stand on the highest pavement of the stair—
Lean on a garden urn—
Weave, weave the sunlight in your hair—
Clasp your flowers to you with a pained surprise—
5   Fling them to the ground and turn
With a fugitive resentment in your eyes:
But weave, weave the sunlight in your hair.

So I would have had him leave,
So I would have had her stand and grieve,
10   So he would have left
As the soul leaves the body torn and bruised,
As the mind deserts the body it has used.
I should find
Some way incomparably light and deft,
15   Some way we both should understand,
Simple and faithless as a smile[3] and shake of the hand.

She turned away, but with the autumn weather
Compelled my imagination many days,
Many days and many hours:
20   Her hair over her arms and her arms full of flowers.
And I wonder how they should have been together!
I should have lost a gesture and a pose.
Sometimes these cogitations still amaze
The troubled midnight and the noon's repose.

28

POEMS
1920

GERONTION[1]

Thou hast nor youth nor age
But as it were an after dinner sleep
Dreaming of both.[2]

Here I am, an old man in a dry month,
Being read to by a boy, waiting for rain.[3]
I was neither at the hot gates[4]
Nor fought in the warm rain
5   Nor knee deep in the salt marsh, heaving a cutlass,
Bitten by flies, fought.
My house is a decayed house,
And the Jew[5] squats on the window-sill, the owner,
Spawned in some estaminet[6] of Antwerp,
10 Blistered in Brussels, patched and peeled in London.
The goat coughs at night in the field overhead;
Rocks, moss, stonecrop,[7] iron, merds.[8]
The woman keeps the kitchen,[9] makes tea,
Sneezes at evening, poking the peevish gutter.[10]
15   I an old man,
A dull head among windy spaces.

Signs are taken for wonders. "We would see a sign!"[11]
The word within a word, unable to speak a word,[12]
Swaddled[13] with darkness. In the juvescence of the
    year
20 Came Christ the tiger

In depraved May,[14] dogwood and chestnut, flowering
   judas,
To be eaten, to be divided, to be drunk[15]
Among whispers; by Mr. Silvero[16]
With caressing hands, at Limoges[17]
25   Who walked all night in the next room;
By Hakagawa, bowing among the Titians;
By Madame de Tornquist, in the dark room
Shifting the candles; Fräulein von Kulp
Who turned in the hall, one hand on the door.
   Vacant shuttles
30   Weave the wind.[18] I have no ghosts,
An old man in a draughty house
Under a windy knob.[19]

After such knowledge, what forgiveness?[20] Think now
History has many cunning passages, contrived
   corridors
35   And issues, deceives with whispering ambitions,
Guides us by vanities. Think now
She gives when our attention is distracted
And what she gives, gives with such supple confusions
That the giving famishes the craving. Gives too late
40   What's not believed in, or if still believed,
In memory only, reconsidered passion. Gives too soon
Into weak hands,[21] what's thought can be dispensed
   with
Till the refusal propagates a fear. Think
Neither fear nor courage saves us. Unnatural vices
45   Are fathered by our heroism. Virtues
Are forced upon us by our impudent crimes.

These tears are shaken from the wrath-bearing tree.[22]

The tiger springs in the new year. Us he devours.
   Think at last
We have not reached conclusion, when I
50   Stiffen in a rented house. Think at last
I have not made this show purposelessly
And it is not by any concitation[23]
Of the backward devils.
I would meet you upon this honestly.
55   I that was near your heart was removed therefrom[24]
To lose beauty in terror, terror in inquisition.
I have lost my passion: why should I need to keep it
Since what is kept must be adulterated?
I have lost my sight, smell, hearing, taste and touch:
60   How should I use them for your closer contact?

These[25] with a thousand small deliberations
Protract the profit of their chilled delirium,
Excite the membrane, when the sense has cooled,
With pungent sauces, multiply variety
65   In a wilderness of mirrors.[26] What will the spider do,
Suspend its operations, will the weevil
Delay? De Bailhache, Fresca, Mrs. Cammel, whirled
Beyond the circuit of the shuddering Bear
In fractured atoms.[27] Gull against the wind, in the
   windy straits
70   Of Belle Isle,[28] or running on the Horn.
White feathers in the snow, the Gulf[29] claims,
And an old man driven on the Trades[30]
To a sleepy corner.

                       Tenants of the house,
75   Thoughts of a dry brain in a dry season.

BURBANK WITH A BAEDEKER:
BLEISTEIN WITH A CIGAR

Tra-la-la-la-la-la-laire—nil nisi divinum stabile est;
caetera fumus—the gondola stopped, the old palace
was there, how charming its grey and pink—goats and
monkeys, with such hair too!—so the countess passed
on until she came through the little park, where Niobe
presented her with a cabinet, and so departed.[1]

Burbank crossed a little bridge
    Descending[2] at a small hotel;
Princess Volupine arrived,
    They were together, and he fell.[3]

5   Defunctive[4] music under sea
    Passed seaward with the passing bell[5]
Slowly: the God Hercules
    Had left him, that had loved him well.[6]

The horses, under the axletree[7]
10   Beat up[8] the dawn from Istria
With even feet.[9] Her shuttered barge
    Burned on the water all the day.[10]

But this or such was Bleistein's[11] way:
    A saggy bending of the knees
15   And elbows, with the palms turned out,
    Chicago Semite Viennese.

A lustreless protrusive eye
    Stares from the protozoic[12] slime
At a perspective of Canaletto.[13]
20   The smoky candle end of time

Declines. On the Rialto[14] once.
    The rats are underneath the piles.
The Jew is underneath the lot.[15]
    Money in furs. The boatman smiles,

25 Princess Volupine extends
    A meagre,[16] blue-nailed, phthisic[17] hand
To climb the waterstair. Lights, lights,[18]
    She entertains Sir Ferdinand

Klein.[19] Who clipped the lion's wings[20]
30   And flea'd his rump and pared his claws?
Thought Burbank, meditating on
    Time's ruins, and the seven laws.[21]

SWEENEY ERECT

And the trees about me,
Let them be dry and leafless; let the rocks
Groan with continual surges; and behind me
Make all a desolation. Look, look, wenches![1]

Paint me a cavernous waste shore[2]
    Cast in the unstilled Cyclades,[3]
Paint me the bold anfractuous[4] rocks
    Faced by the snarled and yelping seas.

5   Display me Aeolus[5] above
    Reviewing the insurgent gales
Which tangle Ariande's hair
    And swell with haste the perjured sails.

Morning stirs the feet and hands
10   (Nausicaa and Polypheme[6]).
Gesture of orang-outang[7]
    Rises from the sheets in steam.

This withered root of knots of hair
    Slitted below and gashed with eyes,
15   This oval O cropped out with teeth:
    The sickle motion from the thighs

Jackknifes upward at the knees
    Then straightens out from heel to hip

Pushing the framework of the bed
20   And clawing at the pillow slip.[8]

Sweeney addressed full length to shave
        Broadbottomed, pink from nape to base,
Knows the female temperament
        And wipes the suds around his face.

25   (The lengthened shadow of a man
        Is history, said Emerson[9]
Who had not seen the silhouette
        Of Sweeney straddled in the sun.)

Tests the razor on his leg
30   Waiting until the shriek subsides.
The epileptic on the bed
        Curves backward, clutching at her sides.

The ladies of the corridor
        Find themselves involved, disgraced,
35   Call witness to their principles
        And deprecate the lack of taste

Observing that hysteria
        Might easily be misunderstood;
Mrs. Turner intimates
40   It does the house no sort of good.

But Doris, towelled from the bath,
        Enters padding on broad feet,
Bringing sal volatile
        And a glass of brandy neat.

A COOKING EGG[1]

Pipit sate[3] upright in her chair
    Some distance from where I was sitting;
Views of Oxford Colleges
    Lay on the table with the knitting.

5   Daguerreotypes[4] and silhouettes,
    Her grandfather and great great aunts,
Supported on the mantelpiece
    An *Invitation to the Dance*.[5]

      •   •   •   •

I shall not want[6] Honour in Heaven
10   For I shall meet Sir Philip Sidney
And have talk with Coriolanus
    And other heroes of that kidney.[7]

I shall not want[8] Capital in Heaven
    For I shall meet Sir Alfred Mond.[9]
15   We two shall lie together, lapt
    In a five per cent. Exchequer Bond.

I shall not want Society in Heaven,
    Lucretia Borgia[10] shall be my Bride;
Her anecdotes will be more amusing
20   Than Pipit's experience could provide.

I shall not want Pipit in Heaven:
    Madame Blavatsky[11] will instruct me
In the Seven Sacred Trances;[12]
    Piccarda de Donati will conduct me.[13]

     •   •   •   •

25   But where is the penny world[14] I bought
       To eat with Pipit behind the screen?
    The red-eyed scavengers are creeping
       From Kentish Town and Golder's Green;[15]

Where are the eagles and the trumpets?[16]

30   Buried beneath some snow-deep Alps.
    Over buttered scones and crumpets
       Weeping, weeping multitudes
    Droop in a hundred A.B.C.'s.[17]

LE DIRECTEUR[1]

Malheur à la malheureuse Tamise!
Qui coule si près du Spectateur.
Le directeur
Conservateur
5   Du Spectateur
Empeste la brise.
Les actionnaires
Réactionnaires
Du Spectateur
10   Conservateur
Bras dessus bras dessous
Font des tours
A pas de loup.
Dans un égout
15   Une petite fille
En guenilles
Camarde
Regarde
Le directeur
20   Du Spectateur
Conservateur
Et crève d'amour.

MÉLANGE ADULTÈRE DE TOUT[1]

En Amérique, professeur;
En Angleterre, journaliste;
C'est à grands pas et en sueur
Que vous suivrez à peine ma piste.
5   En Yorkshire, conférencier;
A Londres, un peu banquier,
Vous me paierez bien la tête.
C'est à Paris que je me coiffe
Casque noir de jemenfoutiste.
10   En Allemagne, philosophe
Surexcité par Emporheben
Au grand air de Bergsteigleben;
J'erre toujours de-ci de-là
A divers coups de tra là là
15   De Damas jusqu' à Omaha;
Je célébrai mon jour de fête
Dans une oasis d'Afrique
Vêtu d'une peau de girafe.

On montrera mon cénotaphe
20   Aux côtes brûlantes de Mozambique.

LUNE DE MIEL[1]

Ils ont vu les Pay-Bas, ils rentrent à Terre Haute;
Mais une nuit d'été, les voici à Ravenne,
A l'aise entre deux draps, chez deux centaines de
    punaises;
La sueur aestivale, et une forte odeur de chienne.
5   Ils restent sur le dos écartant les genoux
De quatre jambes molles tout gonflées de morsures.
On relève le drap pour mieux égratigner.
Moins d'une lieue d'ici est Saint Apollinaire
En Classe, basilique connue des amateurs
10   De chapitaux d'acanthe que tournoie le vent.

Ils vont prendre le train de huit heures
Prolonger leurs misères de Padoue à Milan
Où se trouve la Cène, et un restaurant pas cher.
Lui pense aux pourboires, et rédige son bilan.
15   Ils auront vu la Suisse et traversé la France.
Et Saint Apollinaire, raide et ascétique,
Vieille usine désaffectée de Dieu, tient encore
Dans ses pierres écroulantes la forme précise de
    Byzance.

THE HIPPOPOTAMUS

*And when this epistle is read among you, cause that
it be read also in the church of the Laodiceans.*[1]

The broad-backed hippopotamus
Rests on his belly in the mud;
Although he seems so firm to us
He is merely flesh and blood.[2]

5   Flesh and blood is weak and frail,
Susceptible to nervous shock;
While the True Church can never fail
For it is based upon a rock.[3]

The hippo's feeble steps may err
10   In compassing material ends,
While the True Church need never stir
To gather in its dividends.

The 'potamus can never reach
The mango on the mango-tree;
15   But fruits of pomegranate and peach
Refresh the Church from over sea.

At mating time the hippo's voice
Betrays inflexions hoarse and odd,
But every week we hear rejoice
20   The Church, at being one with God.

The hippopotamus's day
Is passed in sleep; at night he hunts;
God works in a mysterious way[4]—
The Church can sleep and feed at once.

25   I saw the 'potamus take wing
Ascending from the damp savannas,
And quiring angels round him sing
The praise of God, in loud hosannas.

Blood of the Lamb[5] shall wash him clean
30   And him shall heavenly arms enfold,
Among the saints he shall be seen
Performing on a harp of gold.

He shall be washed as white as snow,
By all the martyr'd virgins kist,
35   While the True Church remains below
Wrapt in the old miasmal[6] mist.

DANS LE RESTAURANT[1]

Le garçon délabré qui n'a rien à faire
Que de se gratter les doigts et se pencher sur mon
    épaule:
    "Dans mon pays il fera temps pluvieux,
    Du vent, du grand soleil, et de la pluie;
5   C'est ce qu'on appelle le jour de lessive des
    gueux."
(Bavard, baveux, à la croupe arrondie,
Je te prie, au moins, ne bave pas dans la soupe).
  "Les saules trempés, et des bourgeons sur les ronces—
    C'est là, dans une averse, qu'on s'abrite.
10 J'avais sept ans, elle était plus petite.
    Ellé était toute mouillée, je lui ai donné des
    primevères."
Les taches de son gilet montent au chiffre de trente-
    huit.
    "Je la chatouillais, pour la fair rire.
    Elle avait une odeur fraîche, qui m'était inconnue."
15 Mais alors, vieux lubrique, à cet âge . . .
  "Monsieur, le fait est dur.
    Il est venu, nous peloter, un gros chien;
    Moi j'avais peur, je l'ai quittée à mi-chemin.
    C'est dommage."
20   Mais alors, tu as ton vautour[2]!
Va t'en te décrotter les rides du visage;
Tiens, ma fourchette, décrasse-toi le crâne.
De quel droit payes-tu des expériences comme moi?
Tiens, voilà dix sous, pour la salle-de-bains.

25   Phlébas, le Phénicien, pendant quinze jours noyé,

Oubliait les cris des mouettes et la houle de
        Cornouaille,
Et les profits et les pertes, et la cargaison d'étain:
Un courant de sous-mer l'emporta trés loin,
Le repassant aux étapes de sa vie antérieure.
30   Figurez-vous donc, c'était un sort pénible;
Cependant, ce fut jadis un bel homme, de haute taille.

Webster[1] was much possessed by death
And saw the skull beneath the skin;
And breastless creatures under ground
Leaned backward with a lipless grin.

5   Daffodil bulbs instead of balls
Stared from the sockets of the eyes![2]
He knew that thought clings round dead limbs
Tightening its lusts and luxuries.

Donne,[3] I suppose, was such another
10   Who found no substitute for sense,
To seize and clutch and penetrate;
Expert beyond experience,

He knew the anguish of the marrow
The ague of the skeleton;
15   No contact possible to flesh
Allayed the fever of the bone.

       .   .   .   .

Grishkin[4] is nice: her Russian eye
Is underlined for emphasis;
Uncorseted, her friendly bust
20   Gives promise of pneumatic bliss.[5]

The couched Brazilian jaguar
Compels the scampering marmoset
With subtle effluence of cat;
Grishkin has a maisonnette;

25   The sleek Brazilian jaguar
      Does not in its arboreal gloom
      Distil so rank a feline smell
      As Grishkin in a drawing-room.

      And even the Abstract Entities[6]
30   Circumambulate her charm;
      But our lot crawls between dry ribs
      To keep our metaphysics warm.

Look, look, master, here comes two religious caterpillars.[1]
THE JEW OF MALTA

Polyphiloprogenitive[2]
The sapient sutlers[3] of the Lord
Drift across the window-panes.
In the beginning was the Word.[4]

In the beginning was the Word.
Superfetation of τὸ ἕν,[5]
And at the mensual[6] turn of time
Produced enervate Origen.[7]

A painter of the Umbrian school[8]
Designed upon a gesso[9] ground
The nimbus of the Baptized God.
The wilderness is cracked and browned.

But through the water pale and thin
Still shine the unoffending feet
And there above the painter set
The Father and the Paraclete.[10]

.   .   .   .

The sable presbyters[11] approach
The avenue of penitence;
The young are red and pustular
Clutching piaculative[12] pence.

Under the penitential gates
Sustained by staring Seraphim
Where the souls of the devout
Burn invisible and dim.[13]

25   Along the garden-wall the bees
With hairy bellies pass between
The staminate and pistillate,
Blest office of the epicene.[14]

Sweeney shifts from ham to ham
30   Stirring the water in his bath.
The masters of the subtle schools
Are controversial, polymath.[15]

SWEENEY AMONG THE NIGHTINGALES

ὤμοι, πέπληγμαι καιρίαν πληγὴν ἔσω.[1]

Apeneck Sweeney spreads his knees
Letting his arms hang down to laugh,
The zebra stripes along his jaw
Swelling to maculate[2] giraffe.

The circles of the stormy moon
Slide westward toward the River Plate,
Death and the Raven[3] drift above
And Sweeney guards the hornèd gate.[4]

Gloomy Orion and the Dog[5]
Are veiled; and hushed the shrunken seas;
The person in the Spanish cape
Tries to sit on Sweeney's knees

Slips and pulls the table cloth
Overturns a coffee-cup,
Reorganized upon the floor
She yawns and draws a stocking up;

The silent man in mocha brown
Sprawls at the window-sill and gapes;
The waiter brings in oranges
Bananas figs and hothouse grapes;

The silent vertebrate exhales,
Contracts and concentrates, withdraws;
Rachel *née* Rabinovitch[6]
Tears at the grapes with murderous paws;[7]

25   She and the lady in the cape
Are suspect, thought to be in league;
Therefore the man with heavy eyes
Declines the gambit, shows fatigue,

Leaves the room and reappears
30   Outside the window, leaning in,
Branches of wistaria
Circumscribe a golden grin;

The host with someone indistinct
Converses at the door apart,
35   The nightingales are singing near
The Convent of the Sacred Heart,

And sang within the bloody wood
When Agamemnon cried aloud
And let their liquid siftings fall
40   To stain the stiff dishonoured shroud.

THE WASTE LAND
1922

"*Nam Sibyllam quidem Cumis ego ipse oculis meis*
vidi in ampulla pendere, et cum illi pueri dicerent:
Σίβυλλα τί θέλεις; *respondebat illa:* ἀποθανεῖν θέλω."[1]

FOR EZRA POUND
il miglior fabbro.

I. The Burial of the Dead

April[1] is the cruellest month, breeding
Lilacs out of the dead land, mixing
Memory and desire, stirring
Dull roots with spring rain.
5   Winter kept us warm, covering
Earth in forgetful snow, feeding
A little life with dried tubers.
Summer surprised us, coming over the Starnbergersee[2]
With a shower of rain; we stopped in the colonnade,
10   And went on in sunlight, into the Hofgarten,[3]
And drank coffee, and talked for an hour.
Bin gar keine Russin, stamm' aus Litauen, echt
    deutsch.[4]
And when we were children, staying at the arch-
    duke's,
My cousin's, he took me out on a sled,
15   And I was frightened. He said, Marie,
Marie, hold on tight. And down we went.
In the mountains, there you feel free.
I read, much of the night, and go south in the winter.

What are the roots that clutch, what branches grow
20   Out of this stony rubbish? Son of man,[5]
You cannot say, or guess, for you know only
A heap of broken images,[6] where the sun beats,
And the dead tree gives no shelter, the cricket no
    relief,[7]
And the dry stone no sound of water. Only
25   There is shadow under this red rock,
(Come in under the shadow of this red rock),
And I will show you something different from either
Your shadow at morning striding behind you

Or your shadow at evening rising to meet you;
30 I will show you fear[8] in a handful of dust.[9]

> Frisch weht der Wind
> Der Heimat zu
> Mein Irisch Kind,
> Wo weilest du?[10]

35 "You gave me Hyacinths[11] first a year ago;
"They called me the hyacinth girl."
—Yet when we came back, late, from the hyacinth
  garden,
Your arms full, and your hair wet, I could not
Speak, and my eyes failed, I was neither
40 Living nor dead, and I knew nothing,
Looking into the heart of light, the silence.[12]
Oed' und leer das Meer.[13]

Madame Sosostris,[14] famous clairvoyante,
Had a bad cold, nevertheless
45 Is known to be the wisest woman in Europe,
With a wicked pack of cards.[15] Here, said she,
Is your card, the drowned Phoenician Sailor,
(Those are pearls that were his eyes. Look![16])
Here is Belladonna, the Lady of the Rocks,[17]
50 The lady of situations.
Here is the man with three staves, and here the
  Wheel,
And here is the one-eyed[18] merchant, and this card,
Which is blank, is something he carries on his back,
Which I am forbidden to see. I do not find
55 The Hanged Man. Fear death by water.
I see crowds of people, walking round in a ring.
Thank you. If you see dear Mrs. Equitone,
Tell her I bring the horoscope myself:
One must be so careful these days.

60   Unreal City,
     Under the brown fog of a winter dawn,
     A crowd flowed[19] over London Bridge, so many,
     I had not thought death had undone so many.[20]
     Sighs, short and infrequent, were exhaled,[21]
65   And each man fixed his eyes before his feet.[22]
     Flowed up the hill and down King William Street,
     To where Saint Mary Woolnoth[23] kept the hours
     With a dead sound[24] on the final stroke of nine.
     There I saw one I knew, and stopped him, crying:
         "Stetson!
70   "You who were with me in the ships at Mylae![25]
     "That corpse you planted last year in your garden,
     "Has it begun to sprout? Will it bloom this year?
     "Or has the sudden frost disturbed its bed?
     "O keep the Dog far hence, that's friend to men,
75   "Or with his nails he'll dig it up again![26]
     "You! hypocrite lecteur!—mon semblable,—mon
         frère!"[27]

II. A GAME OF CHESS[1]

     The Chair she sat in, like a burnished throne,[2]
     Glowed on the marble, where the glass
     Held up by standards wrought with fruited vines
80   From which a golden Cupidon peeped out
     (Another hid his eyes behind his wing)
     Doubled the flames of sevenbranched candelabra
     Reflecting light upon the table as
     The glitter of her jewels rose to meet it,
85   From satin cases poured in rich profusion.
     In vials of ivory and coloured glass
     Unstoppered, lurked her strange synthetic perfumes,
     Unguent, powdered, or liquid—troubled, confused

And drowned the sense in odours; stirred by the air
90   That freshened from the window, these ascended
        In fattening the prolonged candle-flames,
        Flung their smoke into the laquearia,[3]
        Stirring the pattern on the coffered ceiling.
        Huge sea-wood fed with copper
95   Burned green and orange, framed by the coloured
            stone,
        In which sad light a carvèd dolphin swam.
        Above the antique mantel was displayed
        As though a window gave upon the sylvan scene[4]
        The change of Philomel,[5] by the barbarous king
100   So rudely forced;[6] yet there the nightingale
        Filled all the desert with inviolable voice
        And still she cried, and still the world pursues,[7]
        "Jug Jug"[8] to dirty ears.
        And other withered stumps of time
105   Were told upon the walls; staring forms
        Leaned out, leaning, hushing the room enclosed.
        Footsteps shuffled on the stair.
        Under the firelight, under the brush, her hair
        Spread out in fiery points
110   Glowed into words, then would be savagely still.

            "My nerves are bad to-night. Yes, bad. Stay with
                me.
            Speak to me. Why do you never speak? Speak.
                What are you thinking of? What thinking?
                    What?
            I never know what you are thinking. Think."

115   I think we are in rats' alley[9]
        Where the dead men lost their bones.

"What is that noise?"
   The wind under the door.[10]
"What is that noise now? What is the wind doing?"
120   Nothing again nothing.
               "Do

You know nothing? Do you see nothing? Do you
  remember
"Nothing?"

I remember
125 Those are pearls that were his eyes.[11]
"Are you alive, or not? Is there nothing in your
  head?"
                But

O O O O that Shakespeherian Rag[12]—
It's so elegant
130 So intelligent
"What shall I do now? What shall I do?
I shall rush out as I am, and walk the street
With my hair down, so. What shall we do
  tomorrow?
What shall we ever do?"
135   The hot water at ten.
And if it rains, a closed car at four.
And we shall play a game of chess,[13]
Pressing lidless eyes and waiting for a knock upon
  the door.

  When Lil's husband got demobbed,[14] I said—
140 I didn't mince my words, I said to her myself,
HURRY UP PLEASE ITS TIME[15]
Now Albert's coming back, make yourself a bit
  smart.

He'll want to know what you done with that money
    he gave you
To get yourself some teeth. He did, I was there.
145   You have them all out, Lil, and get a nice set,
He said, I swear, I can't bear to look at you.
And no more can't I, I said, and think of poor
    Albert,
He's been in the army four years,[16] he wants a good
    time,
And if you don't give it him, there's others will, I
    said.
150   Oh is there, she said. Something o' that, I said.
Then I'll know who to thank, she said, and give me
    a straight look.
HURRY UP PLEASE ITS TIME
If you don't like it you can get on with it,[17] I said.
Others can pick and choose if you can't.
155   But if Albert makes off, it won't be for lack of
    telling.
You ought to be ashamed, I said, to look so antique.
(And her only thirty-one.)
I can't help it, she said, pulling a long face,
It's them pills I took, to bring it off,[18] she said.
160   (She's had five already, and nearly died of young
    George.)
The chemist[19] said it would be all right, but I've
    never been the same.
You *are* a proper fool, I said.
Well, if Albert won't leave you alone, there it is, I
    said,
What you get married for if you don't want
    children?
165   HURRY UP PLEASE ITS TIME
Well, that Sunday Albert was home, they had a hot
    gammon,[20]

And they asked me in to dinner, to get the beauty of
   it hot—
HURRY UP PLEASE ITS TIME
HURRY UP PLEASE ITS TIME
170 Goonight Bill. Goonight Lou. Goonight May.
   Goonight.
Ta ta. Goonight. Goonight.
Good night, ladies,[21] good night, sweet ladies, good
   night, good night.

III. THE FIRE SERMON[1]

   The river's tent is broken; the last fingers of leaf
Clutch and sink into the wet bank. The wind
175 Crosses the brown land, unheard. The nymphs are
   departed.
Sweet Thames, run softly, till I end my song.
The river bears no empty bottles, sandwich papers,
Silk handkerchiefs, cardboard boxes, cigarette ends
Or other testimony of summer nights. The nymphs
   are departed.[2]
180 And their friends, the loitering[3] heirs of City
   directors;
Departed, have left no addresses.
By the waters of Leman I sat down and wept . . .[4]
Sweet Thames, run softly till I end my song,
Sweet Thames, run softly, for I speak not loud or
   long.
185 But at my back in a cold blast I hear
The rattle of the bones, and chuckle spread from ear
   to ear.[5]

A rat crept softly through the vegetation
Dragging its slimy belly on the bank
While I was fishing in the dull canal

190   On a winter evening round behind the gashouse
      Musing upon the king my brother's wreck
      And on the king my father's death before him.[6]
      White bodies naked on the low damp ground
      And bones cast in a little low dry garret,
195   Rattled by the rat's foot only, year to year.
      But at my back from time to time I hear
      The sound of horns and motors,[7] which shall bring
      Sweeney to Mrs. Porter in the spring.
      O the moon shone bright on Mrs. Porter
200   And on her daughter
      They wash their feet in soda water[8]
      Et O ces voix d'enfants, chantant dans la coupole![9]

      Twit twit twit
      Jug jug jug jug jug jug
205   So rudely forc'd.
      Tereu[10]

      Unreal City[11]
      Under the brown fog of a winter noon
      Mr. Eugenides, the Smyrna merchant[12]
210   Unshaven, with a pocket full of currants
      C.i.f.[13] London: documents at sight,
      Asked me in demotic[14] French
      To luncheon at the Cannon Street Hotel[15]
      Followed by a weekend at the Metropole.[16]

215   At the violet hour,[17] when the eyes and back
      Turn upward from the desk, when the human engine
            waits
      Like a taxi throbbing waiting,
      I Tiresias,[18] though blind, throbbing between two
            lives,

Old man with wrinkled female breasts, can see
220 At the violet hour, the evening hour that strives
Homeward, and brings the sailor home from sea,[19]
The typist home at teatime, clears her breakfast, lights
Her stove, and lays out food in tins.
Out of the window perilously spread
225 Her drying combinations touched by the sun's last
        rays,
On the divan are piled (at night her bed)
Stockings, slippers, camisoles, and stays.
I Tiresias, old man with wrinkled dugs
Perceived the scene, and foretold the rest—
230 I too awaited the expected guest.
He, the young man carbuncular, arrives,
A small house agent's clerk, with one bold stare,
One of the low on whom assurance sits
As a silk hat on a Bradford[20] millionaire.
235 The time is now propitious, as he guesses,
The meal is ended, she is bored and tired,
Endeavours to engage her in caresses
Which still are unreproved, if undesired.
Flushed and decided, he assaults at once;
240 Exploring hands encounter no defence;
His vanity requires no response,
And makes a welcome of indifference.
(And I Tiresias[21] have foresuffered all[22]
Enacted on this same divan or bed;
245 I who have sat by Thebes below the wall
And walked among the lowest of the dead.[23])
Bestows one final patronising kiss,
And gropes his way, finding the stairs unlit . . .

She turns and looks a moment in the glass,
250 Hardly aware of her departed lover;

Her brain allows one half-formed thought to pass:
"Well now that's done: and I'm glad it's over."
When lovely woman stoops to folly[24] and
Paces about her room again, alone,
255　She smooths her hair with automatic hand,
And puts a record on the gramophone.

"This music crept by me upon the waters"[25]
And along the Strand, up Queen Victoria Street.[26]
O City city, I can sometimes hear
260　Beside a public bar in Lower Thames Street,[27]
The pleasant whining of a mandoline
And a clatter and a chatter from within
Where fishmen[28] lounge at noon: where the walls
Of Magnus Martyr hold
265　Inexplicable splendour of Ionian white and gold.[29]

　　　　　　The river sweats[30]
　　　　　　Oil and tar
　　　　　　The barges drift
　　　　　　With the turning tide
270　　　　　Red sails
　　　　　　Wide
　　　　　　To leeward, swing on the heavy spar.
　　　　　　The barges wash
　　　　　　Drifting logs
275　　　　　Down Greenwich reach[31]
　　　　　　Past the Isle of Dogs.[32]
　　　　　　　　　　Weialala leia
　　　　　　　　　　Wallala leialala

　　　　　　Elizabeth and Leicester[33]
280　　　　　Beating oars
　　　　　　The stern was formed
　　　　　　A gilded shell

Red and gold
The brisk swell
285   Rippled both shores
Southwest wind
Carried down stream
The peal of bells
White towers
290   Weialala leia
Wallala leialala

"Trams and dusty trees.[34]
Highbury bore me. Richmond and Kew
Undid me.[35] By Richmond I raised my knees
295   Supine on the floor of a narrow canoe."

"My feet are at Moorgate,[36] and my heart
Under my feet. After the event
He wept. He promised 'a new start.'
I made no comment. What should I resent?"

300   "On Margate[37] Sands.
I can connect
Nothing with nothing.
The broken fingernails of dirty hands.
My people humble people who expect
305   Nothing."
                la la

To Carthage then I came[38]

Burning burning burning burning[39]
O Lord Thou pluckest me out[40]
310   O Lord Thou pluckest

burning

IV. Death by Water[1]

Phlebas the Phoenician, a fortnight dead,
Forgot the cry of gulls, and the deep sea swell
And the profit and loss.

315   A current under sea
Picked his bones in whispers. As he rose and fell
He passed the stages of his age and youth
Entering the whirlpool.

                              Gentile or Jew
320   O you who turn the wheel and look to windward,
Consider Phlebas, who was once handsome and tall
    as you.

V. What the Thunder said

After the torchlight[1] red on sweaty faces
After the frosty silence in the gardens
After the agony in stony places
325   The shouting and the crying
Prison and palace and reverberation
Of thunder of spring over distant mountains
He who was living is now dead
We who were living are now dying
330   With a little patience

Here is no water but only rock
Rock and no water and the sandy road
The road winding above among the mountains
Which are mountains of rock without water
335   If there were only water amongst the rock
Amongst the rock one cannot stop or think
Sweat is dry and feet are in the sand
If there were only water amongst the rock
Dead mountain mouth of carious teeth that cannot
    spit

340   Here one can neither stand nor lie nor sit
      There is not even silence in the mountains
      But dry sterile thunder without rain
      There is not even solitude in the mountains
      But red sullen faces sneer and snarl
345   From doors of mudcracked houses
                                    If there were water
         And no rock
         If there were rock
         And also water
350   And water
         A spring
         A pool among the rock
         If there were the sound of water only
         Not the cicada
355   And dry grass singing
         But sound of water over a rock
         Where the hermit-thrush[2] sings in the pine trees
         Drip drop drip drop drop drop drop
         But there is no water

360   Who is the third who walks always beside you?[3]
      When I count, there are only you and I together
      But when I look ahead up the white road
      There is always another one walking beside you
      Gliding wrapt in a brown mantle, hooded
365   I do not know whether a man or a woman
      —But who is that on the other side of you?

      What is that sound[4] high in the air
      Murmur of maternal lamentation
      Who are those hooded hordes swarming
370   Over endless plains, stumbling in cracked earth
      Ringed by the flat horizon only
      What is the city over the mountains

Cracks and reforms and bursts in the violet air
Falling towers
375   Jerusalem Athens Alexandria
Vienna London
Unreal

A woman[5] drew her long black hair out tight
And fiddled whisper music on those strings
And bats with baby faces in the violet light
380   Whistled, and beat their wings
And crawled head downward down a blackened wall
And upside down in air were towers
Tolling reminiscent bells, that kept the hours
And voices singing out of empty cisterns[6] and
       exhausted wells.

385   In this decayed hole among the mountains
In the faint moonlight, the grass is singing
Over the tumbled graves, about the chapel[7]
There is the empty chapel, only the wind's home.
It has no windows, and the door swings,
390   Dry bones can harm no one.
Only a cock stood on the rooftree
Co co rico co co rico[8]
In a flash of lightning. Then a damp gust
Bringing rain

395   Ganga[9] was sunken, and the limp leaves
Waited for rain, while the black clouds
Gathered far distant, over Himavant.[10]
The jungle crouched, humped in silence.
Then spoke the thunder
400   Da[11]
Datta: what have we given?

My friend, blood shaking my heart
The awful daring of a moment's surrender
Which an age of prudence can never retract
405   By this, and this only, we have existed
Which is not to be found in our obituaries
Or in memories draped by the beneficent spider[12]
Or under seals broken by the lean solicitor
In our empty rooms
410   DA
Dayadhvam: I have heard the key[13]
Turn in the door once and turn once only
We think of the key, each in his prison
Thinking of the key, each confirms a prison
415   Only at nightfall, aethereal rumours
Revive for a moment a broken Coriolanus[14]
DA
Damyata: The boat responded
Gaily, to the hand expert with sail and oar
420   The sea was calm, your heart would have responded
Gaily, when invited, beating obedient
To controlling hands[15]

                              I sat upon the shore
Fishing,[16] with the arid plain behind me
425   Shall I at least set my lands in order?[17]
London Bridge is falling down falling down falling
      down[18]
Poi s'ascose nel foco che gli affina[19]
Quando fiam ceu chelidon[20]—O swallow swallow
Le Prince d'Aquitaine à la tour abolie[21]
430   These fragments I have shored against my ruins
Why then Ile fit you.[22] Hieronymo's mad againe.
Datta. Dayadhvam. Damyata.
                  Shantih shantih shantih[23]

NOTES ON THE WASTE LAND[1]

Not only the title, but the plan and a good deal of the incidental symbolism of the poem were suggested by Miss Jessie L. Weston's book on the Grail legend: *From Ritual to Romance* (Cambridge). Indeed, so deeply am I indebted, Miss Weston's book will elucidate the difficulties of the poem much better than my notes can do; and I recommend it (apart from the great interest of the book itself) to any who think such elucidation of the poem worth the trouble. To another work of anthropology I am indebted in general, one which has influenced our generation profoundly; I mean *The Golden Bough*; I have used especially the two volumes *Adonis, Attis, Osiris*. Anyone who is acquainted with these works will immediately recognise in the poem certain references to vegetation ceremonies.

I. THE BURIAL OF THE DEAD

Line 20. Cf. Ezekiel II, i.

23. Cf. Ecclesiastes XII, v.

31. V. Tristan und Isolde, I, verses 5–8.

42. Id. III, verse 24.

46. I am not familiar with the exact constitution of the Tarot pack of cards, from which I have obviously departed to suit my own convenience. The Hanged Man, a member of the traditional pack, fits my purpose in two ways: because he is associated in my mind with the Hanged God of Frazer, and because I associate him with the hooded figure in the passage of the disciples to Emmaus in Part V. The Phoenician Sailor and the Merchant appear later; also the "crowds of people," and Death by Water is executed in Part IV. The Man with Three Staves (an authentic member of the Tarot pack) I associate, quite arbitrarily, with the Fisher King himself.

60. Cf. Baudelaire:

"Fourmillante cité, cité pleine de rêves,

"Ou le spectre en plein jour raccroche le passant."

63. Cf. Inferno III, 55–57:

> si lunga tratta
> di gente, ch'io non avrei creduto
> che morte tanta n'avesse disfatta.

64. Cf. Inferno IV, 25–27:

Quivi, secondo che per ascoltare,
non avea piante mai che di sospiri
che l'aura eterna facevan tremare.

68. A phenomenon which I have often noticed.

74. Cf. the Dirge in Webster's *White Devil*.

76. V. Baudelaire, Preface to *Fleurs du Mal*.

II. A Game of Chess

77. Cf. *Antony and Cleopatra*, II, ii, l. 190.

92. Laquearia. V. *Aeneid*, I, 726:

dependent lychni laquearibus aureis

incensi, et noctem flammis funalia vincunt.

98. Sylvan scene. V. Milton, *Paradise Lost*, IV, 140.

99. V. Ovid, *Metamorphoses*, VI, Philomela.

100. Cf. Part III, l. 204.

115. Cf. Part III, l. 195.

118. Cf. Webster: "Is the wind in that door still?"

126. Cf. Part I, l. 37, 48.

138. Cf. the game of chess in Middleton's *Women beware Women*.

III. The Fire Sermon

176. V. Spenser, *Prothalamion*.

192. Cf. *The Tempest*, I, ii.

196. Cf. Marvell, *To His Coy Mistress*.

197. Cf. Day, *Parliament of Bees*:

"When of the sudden, listening, you shall hear,
"A noise of horns and hunting, which shall bring
"Actaeon to Diana in the spring,
"Where all shall see her naked skin . . ."

199. I do not know the origin of the ballad from which these lines are taken: it was reported to me from Sydney, Australia.

202. V. Verlaine, *Parsifal*.

210. The currants were quoted at a price "cost insurance and freight to London"; and the Bill of Lading, etc., were to be handed to the buyer upon payment of the sight draft.

218. Tiresias, although a mere spectator and not indeed a "character," is yet the most important personage in the poem, uniting all the rest. Just as the one-eyed merchant seller of currants, melts into the Phoenician Sailor, and the latter is not wholly distinct from Ferdinand Prince of Naples, so all the women are one woman, and the two sexes meet in Tiresias.

What Tiresias *sees*, in fact, is the substance of the poem. The whole passage from Ovid is of great anthropological interest:

. . . Cum Iunone iocos et "maior vestra profecto est
Quam quae contingit maribus," dixisse, "voluptas."
Illa negat; placuit quae sit sententia docti
Quaerere Tiresiae: venus huic erat utraque nota.
Nam duo magnorum viridi coeuntia silva
Corpora serpentum baculi violaverat ictu
Deque viro factus, mirabile, femina septem
Egerat autumnos; octavo rursus eosdem
Vidit et "est vestrae si tanta potentia plagae,"
Dixit "ut auctoris sortem in contraria mutet,
Nunc quoque vos feriam!" percussis anguibus isdem
Forma prior rediit genetivaque venit imago.
Arbiter hic igitur sumptus de lite iocosa
Dicta Iovis firmat; gravius Saturnia iusto
Nec pro materia fertur doluisse suique
ludicis aeterna damnavit lumina nocte,
At pater omnipotens (neque enim licet irrita cuiquam
Facta dei fecisse deo) pro lumine adempto
Scire futura dedit poenamque levavit honore.

221. This may not appear as exact as Sappho's lines, but I had in mind the "longshore" or "dory" fisherman, who returns at nightfall.

253. V. Goldsmith, the song in *The Vicar of Wakefield*.

257. V. *The Tempest*, as above.

264. The interior of St. Magnus Martyr is to my mind one of the finest among Wren's interiors. See *The Proposed Demolition of Nineteen City Churches* (P. S. King & Son, Ltd.).

266. The Song of the (three) Thames-daughters begins here. From line 292 to 306 inclusive they speak in turn. V. *Götterdämmerung*, III, i: the Rhine-daughters.

279. V. Froude, *Elizabeth*, Vol. I, ch. iv, letter of De Quadra to Philip of Spain:

"In the afternoon we were in a barge, watching the games on the river. (The Queen) was alone with Lord Robert and myself on the poop, when they began to talk nonsense, and went so far that Lord Robert at last said, as I was on the spot there was no reason why they should not be married if the queen pleased."

293. Cf. *Purgatorio*, V. 133:

> "Ricorditi di me, che son la Pia;
> "Siena mi fe', disfecemi Maremma."

307. V. St. Augustine's *Confessions*: "to Carthage then I came, where a cauldron of unholy loves sang all about mine ears."

308. The complete text of the Buddha's Fire Sermon (which corresponds in importance to the Sermon on the Mount) from which these words are taken, will be found translated in the late Henry Clarke Warren's *Buddhism in Translation* (Harvard Oriental Series). Mr. Warren was one of the great pioneers of Buddhist studies in the Occident.

309. From St. Augustine's *Confessions* again. The collocation of these two representatives of eastern and western asceticism, as the culmination of this part of the poem, is not an accident.

V. What the Thunder said

In the first part of Part V three themes are employed: the journey to Emmaus, the approach to the Chapel Perilous (see Miss Weston's book) and the present decay of eastern Europe.

357. This is *Turdus aonalaschkae pallasii,* the hermit-thrush which I have heard in Quebec Province. Chapman says (*Handbook of Birds of Eastern North America*) "it is most at home in secluded woodland and thickety retreats. . . . Its notes are not remarkable for variety or volume, but in purity and sweetness of tone and exquisite modulation they are unequalled." Its "water-dripping song" is justly celebrated.

360. The following lines were stimulated by the account of one of the Antarctic expeditions (I forget which, but I think one of Shackleton's): it was related that the party of explorers, at the extremity of their strength, had the constant delusion that there was *one more member* than could actually be counted.

366–76. Cf. Hermann Hesse, *Blick ins Chaos*: "Schon ist halb Europa, schon ist zumindest der halbe Osten Europas auf dem Wege zum Chaos, fährt betrunken im heiligen Wahn am Abgrund entlang und singt dazu, singt betrunken und hymnisch wie Dmitri Karamasoff sang. Ueber diese Lieder lacht der Bürger beleidigt, der Heilige und Seher hört sie mit Tränen."

401. "Datta, dayadhvam, damyata" (Give, sympathise, control). The fable of the meaning of the Thunder is found in the *Brihadaranyaka— Upanishad, 5,* I. A translation is found in Deussen's *Sechzig Upanishads des Veda*, p. 489.

407. Cf. Webster, *The White Devil*, V, vi:

> ". . . they'll remarry
> Ere the worm pierce your winding-sheet, ere the spider
> Make a thin curtain for your epitaphs."

411. Cf. *Inferno*, XXXIII, 46:

> "ed io senti chiavar l'uscio di sotto
> all' orribile torre."

Also F. H. Bradley, *Appearance and Reality*, p. 306.
"My external sensations are no less private to my self than are my thoughts or my feelings. In either case my experience falls within my own circle, a circle closed on the outside; and, with all its elements alike, every sphere is opaque to the others which surround it. . . . In brief, regarded as an existence which appears in a soul, the whole world for each is peculiar and private to that soul."

424. V. Weston: *From Ritual to Romance*; chapter on the Fisher King.

427. V. *Purgatorio*, XXVI, 148.

> " 'Ara vos prec per aquella valor
> 'que vos condus al som de l'escalina,
> 'sovenha vos a temps de ma dolor.'
> Poi s'ascose nel foco che gli affina."

428. V. *Pervigilium Veneris*. Cf. Philomela in Parts II and III.

429. V. Gerard de Nerval, Sonnet *El Desdichado*.

431. V. Kyd's *Spanish Tragedy*.

433. Shantih. Repeated as here, a formal ending to an Upanishad. "The Peace which passeth understanding" is our equivalent to this word.

TEXTUAL NOTES

No attempt has been made at a full collation; these notes merely draw attention to some of the variations between the early and the later texts.

THE LOVE SONG OF J. ALFRED PRUFROCK
   Epigraph 4. perciocchè perciò che] later eds. (after 1944).
   15–34. (omitted in *Poetry* [Chicago])

PORTRAIT OF A LADY
   118. *Doubtful . . . while*], 1917, *Ara Vos Prec Doubtful, for a while*]
later eds.

RHAPSODY ON A WINDY NIGHT
   (Called "Rhapsody of a Windy Night" in BLAST, July 1915)
   5. *floors of the memory*] *floors of memory* later eds.
   29. *Stiff and white*] this line, present in BLAST, is omitted in *Ara Vos
Prec* but included in *Poems* (New York), 1920.
   39. *quay*] *quai* BLAST
   58. *old Cologne*] *eau de Cologne* later eds.

MORNING AT THE WINDOW
   4. *Sprouting*] 1920. *Hanging Poetry*, September 1916.

HYSTERIA
   Omitted from *Ara Vos Prec*, included in *Poems* (New York) 1920, re-
placing a poem called "Ode," which disappeared from the canon.

GERONTION
   8. *Jew*] later eds. *jew Ara Vos Prec* and many others.
   17. *sign.!* 1925+ *sign. Ara Vos Prec* and 1920.
   60. *use them*] later eds; *use it* 1920.
   71. *Gulf*] later eds.; *gulf* 1920.
   72. *on*] *by* later eds.

BURBANK WITH A BAEDEKER
   23. *Jew*] later eds. *jew Ara Vos Prec, Poems* 1920.

SWEENEY ERECT
  26. *said*] *Poems* 1920. *says Ara Vos Prec.*

A COOKING EGG
  32. *Poems*, 1920 has a note on this line: "i.e., an endemic teashop, found in all parts of London. The Initials signify: Aerated Bread Company Limited."

LE DIRECTEUR
  Title: "Le Spectateur," *Ara Vos Prec.*
  1. *Tamise!*] *Ara Vos Prec, Poems*, 1920 *Tamise* later eds.

MÉLANGE ADULTÈRE DU TOUT
  7. in parentheses *Ara Vos Prec*

LUNE DE MIEL
  4. *aestivale*] *Poems*, 1920. *aestival Ara Vos Prec.*
  5. *écartant*] *Ara Vos Prec, Poems*, 1920. *écartent* some later eds. (incorrectly).

THE HIPPOPOTAMUS
  Epigraph] Here printed without the long Latin quotation from St. Ignatius which precedes it in early texts and which was removed from later editions, though ultimately restored. See *Collected Poems 1909–1962* (1963), p. 41.
  13, 25. *'potamus*] *Ara Vos Prec, Poems*, 1920. *potamus Poems*, 1919.

DANS LE RESTAURANT
  14. *Elle . . . fraîche*] *Ara Vos Prec, Poems*, 1920. *J'éprouvais un instant de puissance et de délire Poems* later eds.
  15. *à cet âge*] *Poems*, 1920. omitted in *Ara Vos Prec.*
  24. *salle-de-bains*] *Poems*, 1920. *salle-de bain Ara Vos Prec.*

WHISPERS OF IMMORTALITY
  25–6. *The sleek . . . gloom*] *Poems*, 1920. *The sleek and sinuous jaguar / Does not in his arboreal gloom Ara Vos Prec.*
  29. *Abstract Entities*] *Poems*, 1920. *And even the abstracter entities Ara Vos Prec.*
  32. *our*] *Poems*, 1920. *its Ara Vos Prec.*

Mr. Eliot's Sunday Morning Service

Epigraph as in *Poems*, 1920. *here comes two of the religious caterpillars* Ara Vos Prec and *Little Review*, September 1918.

Sweeney Among the Nightingales

epigraph] followed in *Poems*, 1919, *Ara Vos Prec* and *Poems*, 1920 by the translation, which is omitted in later editions.

21. *exhales*] *Ara Vos Prec*, *Poems*, 1920. *in brown* later eds.

39. *siftings*] *Little Review* September 1918 and later eds. *droppings* Ara Vos Prec, *Poems*, 1920.

The Waste Land

The present text, except for the author's notes, which first appeared in the Boni & Liveright edition in December 1922, is that of the earliest American publication in *The Dial*, November 1922, shortly after its first British publication in *The Criterion*, October 1922. An editorial note in *The Dial* explains that "an edition of *The Waste Land* will presently be issued by Boni & Liveright." The text has varied little since its first publication.

epigraph] See note.

79. *Held up*] *Sustained Criterion.*

335. *If there were only water amongst the rock*] *Dial If there were water we should stop and drink Criterion and later eds.*

428. ceu *Dial* and *Criterion*, ed. of 1922 uti later eds.

PRUFROCK AND OTHER OBSERVATIONS (1917)

This first collection was published in 1917 by the Egoist Press, London (five hundred copies). Ezra Pound, at this time Eliot's keenest advocate, secretly contributed five pounds (borrowed) to the cost of printing. For surviving but rejected earlier poems see T. S. Eliot, *Inventions of the March Hare: Poems 1909–1917*, ed. Christopher Ricks (1996), and *Poems Written in Early Youth* (1950, 1967). According to information provided by Eliot's friend John Hayward to the poet's French translator Pierre Leyris (*Poèmes 1910–30* [1947]), the earliest of the poems in this volume was "Portrait of a Lady," begun in early 1910 and finished in November 1911, when the poet was twenty-three.

1. *Dedication:* Jean Verdenal, poet and medical man, was killed in the Dardanelles campaign in 1915, aged twenty-five. He was a very close friend of Eliot during his time in Paris. The dedication appeared in *Prufrock and Other Observations* (1917), was dropped in the editions of 1920, and restored, with the addition of the words "mort aux Dardanelles," in *Poems 1909–1925* (1925), where dedication and epigraph first appeared together, as presumably Eliot had intended.

2. *Epigraph*: from Dante, *Purgatorio*, XXI.133–136: "Now you can understand the quantity of love that warms me to you, when our vanity is forgotten, treating shadows like a solid thing."

THE LOVE SONG OF J. ALFRED PRUFROCK

First published in *Poetry*, Chicago, in June 1915, "Prufrock" is reported by Leyris to have been mostly written in 1911, when Eliot was in Paris and Munich; but the poet himself stated that when he went to Paris to study in the fall of 1910 the poem was already "conceived" and that "several fragments" existed "which were ultimately embodied in the poem"—probably the lines beginning "I am not Prince Hamlet" among them. Another section, entitled "Prufrock's Pervigilium" ("Prufrock's Vigil"), was written, probably in 1912, but this was dropped. It is now to be found in Ricks, pp. 43–4.

1. *Epigraph:* from Dante, *Inferno*, XXVII.61–66: "If I thought that my reply would be to a person who would ever return to the world, this flame would remain without more movement. But since no one has ever returned alive from this deep, if what I hear is true, I can answer you without fear of infamy." The speaker, Guido da Montrefelto, is wrapped in a flame which trembles when he speaks. In his own way Prufrock is making his confession to people who are similarly trapped.

2. *etherised:* anesthetized.

3. *In the room . . .:* Borrowed from Jules Laforgue, a strong influence on Eliot at this time: "Dans la pièce les femmes vont et viennent, / En parlant des maîtres de Sienne" ("In the room the women come and go, / Talking of the Siennese masters").

4. *there will be time:* recalling Ecclesiastes 3:1–7.

5. *a dying fall:* Twelfth Night I.i.4.

6. *Is it perfume from a dress:* Manuscript in Eliot's Notebook has "Is it the skin or perfume . . ." (Ricks, p. 41).

7. The allusion is to the story of Salome and Saint John the Baptist (Mark 6:17–29).

8. *To have squeezed . . .:* cf. Marvell, "To His Coy Mistress": "Let us roll all our strength and all / Our sweetness up into one ball . . ."

9. *Lazarus:* resurrected; see John 11:1–44.

10. *progress:* "A state journey made by a royal or noble personage . . . A state procession" (*OED*).

11. *no doubt:* "withal, an" (*Poetry*, Chicago).

12. *Politic:* scheming, diplomatic (probably with Polonius in mind).

13. *high sentence:* lofty moralizing (as in Chaucer's Clerk of Oxenford, *General Prologue* to *The Canterbury Tales*, line 306).

14. *the Fool:* in Elizabethan drama the Fool was licensed not only to clown but to quibble with his betters.

15. *trousers rolled:* probably referring to the new fashion of turned-up cuffs.

16. *part . . . behind:* a daring new hairstyle?

17. *mermaids singing:* cf. Donne, "Go and catch a falling star," line 5: "Teach me to hear mermaids singing," part of a catalog of impossibilities.

PORTRAIT OF A LADY

Written in installments, February and November 1910, November 1911. Published in *Others* (New York) September 1915.

1. *Epigraph:* Marlowe, *The Jew of Malta*, IV.i.40–42.

2. *Preludes:* by Chopin.

3. cauchemar: nightmare (French).
4. *buried life:* title of a poem by Matthew Arnold.

PRELUDES

I and II written at Harvard, October 1910; III in Paris, 1910–11; IV at Harvard, November 1911. Published in Wyndham Lewis's BLAST (second and final issue), July 1915. Eliot stated that in III he was indebted to Charles-Louis Philippe's novel *Bubu of Montparnasse* (see note on "Rhapsody on a Windy Night," below).

RHAPSODY ON A WINDY NIGHT

Written Paris, March 1911, published BLAST, July 1915.
1. *Beats like . . . .:* cf. Oscar Wilde, "Ballad of Reading Gaol," lines 377–378: "But each man's heart beat thick, and quick, / Like a madman on a drum!"
2. *Regard:* look at (an affected usage from the French, not out of place in a poem so conscious of its French origins). See also lines 35, 50, 65.
3. *see nothing . . .:* cf. Laforgue, "Pierrots": "ces yeux! mais rien n'existe / Derrière" ("These eyes! / But there is nothing behind them").
4. "The moon bears no grudge": based on a line of Laforgue's.
5. *Smells . . . .:* Adapted from an expression in *Marie Donadieu*, a novel by Charles-Louis Philippe: "des odeurs de filles publiques mêlées à des odeurs de nourriture" ("smells of prostitutes mingled with smells of food"). Eliot admired this author, especially for his *Bubu de Montparnasse* (1901), also concerned with Parisian lowlife; in 1932 he wrote a preface to an English translation of the novel.
6. *shoes at the door:* Until quite recently one left one's shoes outside the hotel-room door for the "boots" to clean before morning. (This may suggest a rather better class of hotel than might have been expected in the circumstances.)

MORNING AT THE WINDOW

Written in Oxford, 1915, first published *Poetry* (Chicago), September 1916, where the housemaids are "hanging," not "sprouting"; in a version Pound saw they were "drooping."

THE BOSTON EVENING TRANSCRIPT

Written October 1915, first published *Poetry* (Chicago), October 1915.

1. *La Rochefaucauld:* François de Marsillac, duc de, (1613–80), author of *Réflexions ou sentences et maximes morales* (*Reflections or Adages and Moral Maxims*) 1665, a collection of concise and often cynical aphorisms.

AUNT HELEN

Written October 1915, first published *Poetry* (Chicago), October 1915.

1. *silence in heaven:* cf. Revelation 8:1: "And when he had opened the seventh seal, there was silence in heaven about the space of half an hour."

2. *The Dresden clock:* presumably a clock in a case of delicate Dresden porcelain.

COUSIN NANCY

Written October 1915, first published *Poetry* (Chicago), October 1915.

1. *Matthew and Waldo:* Matthew Arnold (1822–88) and Ralph Waldo Emerson (1803–82).

2. *The army of unalterable law:* cf. George Meredith, "Lucifer in Starlight": "Around the ancient track marched, rank on rank, / The army of unalterable law."

MR. APOLLINAX

Written September 1916, first published *Poetry* (Chicago), September 1916. A satirical portrait of the philosopher Bertrand Russell (1872–1970), seen in the sedate academic environment of contemporary Harvard, where Russell taught Eliot in 1914. Later they became, not altogether happily, quite intimate.

1. *Epigraph:* "Such novelty! Heavens, what paradoxes! How inventive he is!" from *Zeuxis*, a dialogue of Lucian (2nd cent. C.E.) quoted in Charles Whibley's *Studies in Frankness* (1898). Lucian is condemning ostentatious cleverness; when Eliot saw the words quoted by Whibley (p. 217n.) he presumably thought of Russell.

2. *Fragilion:* invented name for a figure the opposite of the ebullient Apollinax.

3. *Priapus:* classical phallic god, presiding over fertility, and often a garden statue.

4. *worried bodies . . .:* from the *Bateau Ivre* (*Drunken Boat*) of Arthur Rimbaud (1854–91): "entranced and pallid flotsam, a dreaming

drowned man sometimes goes down" (translation of Oliver Bernard, 1962).

HYSTERIA

Written November 1915, first published in *Prufrock and Other Observations* (1917).

CONVERSATION GALANTE

Written September 1916, first published *Poetry* (Chicago), September 1916. It is based on Laforgue's poem "Autre Complainte de Lord Pierrot."

1. *Prester John:* medieval legendary figure supposed to have ruled the extreme Orient.

LA FIGLIA CHE PIANGE

Written September 1916, first published *Poetry* (Chicago), September 1916. According to his friend John Hayward, the origin of this poem was an unsuccessful search for a statue in a museum in north Italy (Helen Gardner, *The Art of T. S. Eliot*, 6th impression [1968], p. 107 n. 2).

1. *Title:* "Young Girl Weeping."
2. *Epigraph:* Virgil, *Aeneid*, I.327: "What should I call thee, maiden?"
3. *Simple and faithless:* from Laforgue, "Pétition": "simple et sans foi comme un bonjour" ("simple and faithless as a 'good-day' ").

POEMS 1920.

Published by Knopf, New York, 1920, this volume is almost identical in content with *Ara Vos Prec*, published in a limited edition by the Ovid Press, London, in the same month (February), though the order of the poems is different. Several of the poems (but not "Gerontion") had appeared in *Poems by T. S. Eliot*, published at the Hogarth Press by Leonard and Virginia Woolf, 1919.

GERONTION:

Begun 1917, finished 1919, first published 1920. Eliot considered making it a prologue to *The Waste Land*, but was dissuaded by Ezra Pound.

1. *Title:* "Little old man" in Greek.
2. *Epigraph:* Shakespeare, *Measure for Measure*, III.i.32–34 ("dinner's

sleep," "dreaming on both"). The Duke is advising Claudio to take the prospect of death calmly; Claudio at first accepts his counsel, but later gives way to a dread of what happens after death: "to be imprisoned in the viewless winds / And blown with restless violence round about / The pendent world" (lines 123–125)—lines which are echoed in lines 67–69 below.

3. *Here I am . . .:* As Eliot remarked, these lines derive from A. C. Benson's biography (1905) of Edward FitzGerald, the translator of Omar Khayyàm, whose *Rubaiyat,* in FitzGerald's translation, had been important to the adolescent Eliot: "here he sits, in a dry month, old and blind, being read to by a country boy, longing for rain." An argument for the profound effect of FitzGerald's poem, and Benson's biography, on Eliot, especially at this time, can be found in Vinnie-Marie D'Ambrosio, *Eliot Possessed: T. S. Eliot and FitzGerald's "Rubaiyat"* (1989).

4. *hot gates:* Greek "Thermopylae," literally translated. This was a militarily important pass.

5. *Jew:* only in later editions given an uppercase J.

6. *estaminet:* tavern, dive.

7. *stonecrop: Sedum acre,* an herb that grows on rocks and old walls.

8. *merds:* excrements.

9. *woman . . . kitchen:* echoing another letter of FitzGerald's.

10. *gutter:* presumably "sink" (*OED,* s.v.3c), though some think it adapted from German "gitter," the fender, grill, etc. of an open fire.

11. *Signs . . . sign!":* NT uses Greek *teras,* "portent, marvel, wonder" in combination with *semeion,* "sign, miracle, remarkable event." The Pharisees say to Jesus, "Master, we would have a sign from thee." He replies, "An evil and adulterous generation seeketh after a sign" (Matt. 12:38–39). In John 4:48 Jesus says, "Except ye see signs and wonders, ye will not believe."

12. *The word . . . word:* taken from a Nativity Sermon by Bishop Lancelot Andrewes, 1618: "signs are taken for wonders. 'Master, we would fain see a sign,' that is, a miracle. . . . Indeed, every word here [in his text, Luke 2:12–14] is a wonder. . . . *Verbum infans,* the Word without a word; the eternal Word not able to speak a word . . ." Eliot seems to have mistaken Andrewes's sense in writing "within a word," and he repeats the error in his essay "For Lancelot Andrewes" (1926), finally getting it right in *Ash-Wednesday* (1930), where line 153 reads, "The Word without a word, the Word unheard."

13. *Swaddled:* also from Andrewes's sermon ("swaddling clothes," in

Luke 2:7 (King James Version). *Juvescence,* properly "juvenescence," "the state of becoming young"—i.e., spring. The form used by Eliot is the earliest recorded in *OED.*

14. *depraved May:* a concentrated allusion to a passage in Henry Adams, *The Education of Henry Adams* (1918).

15. *To be eaten . . .:* the reference is to the Eucharist.

16. *Mr. Silvero; Hakagawa, Mme de Tornquist, Fr. von Kulp:* the proper names are inventions, to which we can give such significance as we wish.

17. *Limoges:* French town, famous for china.

18. *vacant shuttles . . . wind:* perhaps remembering Joyce's *Ulysses,* published 1922 but already known to Eliot ("The void awaits surely all them that weave the wind," Section I, near the beginning). "My days are swifter than a weaver's shuttle, and are spent without hope. O remember that my life is wind: mine eye shall no more see good" (Job 7:6–7).

19. *knob:* hill.

20. *After such . . . 11. 33 ff.:* a (highly original) pastiche of Jacobean dramatic verse, in which Eliot was keenly interested at the time.

21. *Too soon / Into weak hands:* Shelley, *Adonais,* 257, "Too soon, and with weak hands."

22. *wrath-bearing tree:* cf. Blake's "A Poison Tree," where anger produces a tree watered by tears.

23. *Concitation:* stirring up, rousing (an archaism).

24. *I that was . . .:* based on Middleton, *The Changeling* (1624), V.iii.150–151: "I am that of your blood was taken from you / For your better health." The editions Eliot used had the inferior reading "I that am of your blood . . ." He praised the passage in an essay on Middleton (1927, *Selected Essays,* p. 169).

25. *These:* people lost in sensuality.

26. *wilderness of mirrors:* acknowledged to be a reminiscence of Ben Jonson, *The Alchemist* (1612), II.ii.45–48, quoted by Eliot in an essay on Jonson (1919) in *Selected Essays* (1932), pp. 147ff. Perhaps also a reminiscence of "a wilderness of monkeys," Shakespeare, *The Merchant of Venice,* III.i.122.

27. *whirled / Beyond the circuit . . .:* based on the dying speech of Bussy in George Chapman's *Bussy d'Ambois* (1607), V.iv: "fly where men feel / The burning axletree, and those that suffer / Beneath the chariot of the snowy Bear . . ." See Eliot's comments in *The Use of Poetry and the Use of Criticism* (1933), pp. 146–7, where he remarks that the

passage, which had meant much to him, evidently meant much also to Seneca, the Roman playwright, from whom Chapman derived it. The names are made up, and are as if from a society column; they suffer the fate foreseen by Claudio in *Measure for Measure*. "Fresca" figures in a pseudo-Popian section of the *Waste Land MS*, canceled by Pound.

28. *Belle Isle:* near Labrador. *Horn:* Cape Horn, the southern tip of South America.

29. *the Gulf:* the warmer waters of the Gulf Stream.

30. *Trades:* Trade winds, blowing constantly from the northeast in the Northern Tropics.

BURBANK WITH A BAEDEKER: BLEISTEIN WITH A CIGAR

Probably written July 1919, first published *Arts and Letters*, summer 1919.

1. *Epigraph:* all the fragments here assembled relate to Venice; the first is from Théophile Gautier's poem "Sur les lagunes," the second from the inscription on a Saint Sebastian by Mantegna in Venice, the third from Henry James's novella *The Aspern Papers; goats and monkeys* is from *Othello*, IV.i.263, and "with such hair too!" from Browning's "A Toccata of Galuppi's," xv. The last fragment is from the closing stage direction of John Marston's *The Noble Lorde and Lady of Huntingdons Entertainment of their Right Noble Mother . . .* (1607).

2. *descending:* a gallicism, roughly "arriving."

3. *They were together . . . :* cf. Tennyson, "The Sisters," line 4: "They were together, and she fell."

4. *Defunctive:* funereal (as in Shakespeare, "The Phoenix and Turtle," line 14).

5. *passing bell:* tolled to commemorate a death.

6. *the God Hercules . . . :* cf. Shakespeare, *Antony and Cleopatra*, IV.iii. Soldiers, hearing "defunctive music," take it as a sign that the god Hercules ("whom Antony loved") is leaving him. (In Shakespeare's source, Plutarch, it is Bacchus whose departure is signaled.) According to Eliot, Hercules signifies sexual virility.

7. *The horses . . . :* The horses are those of the sun; the axletree is the sky (see note on "Gerontion," I. 68).

8. *Beat up:* perhaps nautical (sailing into the wind), perhaps from hunting (the horses are raising the dawn as beaters raise game).

9. *with even feet:* a famous phrase from Horace, *Odes*, I.iv.13, where death is said to step *aequo pede*, "with equal [impartial] foot."

10. *Her shuttered barge . . . :* for the barge (here presumably a gondola) see Shakespeare, *Antony and Cleopatra*, II.ii.191ff., Enobarbus's description of Cleopatra's barge.

11. *Bleistein:* On the anti-Semitic implications of the name, and the whole question of Eliot's attitude in this respect, see Christopher Ricks, *T.S. Eliot and Prejudice* (1988) and Anthony Julius, *T. S. Eliot and Anti-Semitism* (1995).

12. *protozoic:* referring to the most primitive forms of life.

13. *Canaletto:* Antonio Canale (1697–1768), Venetian painter, famous for his views of Venice.

14. *Rialto:* The ancient business district of Venice. Cf. Shakespeare, *The Merchant of Venice*, I.iii.

15. *The Jew is . . . :* a prejudice echoing that of Mr. Deasey in Joyce's *Ulysses* ("Nestor") and here, according to some, used ironically.

16. *meagre:* thin.

17. *phthisic:* tubercular (usually "phthisical").

18. *Lights, lights:* see *Hamlet*, II.ii.263–264, and *Othello*, I.i.144.

19. *Sir Ferdinand / Klein:* another Jewish name, here presumably of an English Jew.

20. *The lion's wings:* the winged lion of St. Mark, patron saint of Venice.

21. *the seven laws:* obscure; some cite Ruskin's *Seven Lamps of Architecture* (1849) and others a Talmudic compilation of seven commandments.

SWEENEY ERECT

Probably written summer 1919, published with "Burbank," 1920. Sweeney recurs in "Sweeney Among the Nightingales," *The Waste Land*, and *Sweeney Agonistes*. Eliot is reported as having said he was based on a retired boxer who gave him some lessons at Harvard; and on another occasion that he was based on a Boston Irish barman.

1. *Epigraph:* from Beaumont and Fletcher's *The Maid's Tragedy* (1610), II.ii.744–747.

2. *Paint me . . . :* in the passage from *The Maid's Tragedy* Aspatia has been watching her servants portray in needlework the story of Ariadne, left behind when Theseus sailed away. She tells them how to make the picture more tragic by modeling Ariadne on herself: hence "paint me a picture . . ."

3. *Cyclades:* Aegean Islands.

4. *anfractuous:* here, presumably, "hard" and "rugged." (*OED* gives this passage as the first use in English, deriving from French *anfractueux*,

which does mean "craggy." In English the sense is "sinuous, winding, circuitous.")

5. *Aeolus:* Greek god of winds (keeping up the tone of mythological programming begun in the epigraph).

6. *Nausicaa:* daughter of King Alcinous; she was confronted on the beach by the naked Odysseus (Ulysses) when he was cast ashore on her island: Homer, *Odyssey*, VI. *Polypheme:* the Cyclops who captured Odysseus and his men only to be tricked into letting them escape (*Odyssey*, IX).

7. *orang-outan:* "more correctly, 'orang-utan' " (*OED*) a Malay word meaning "man of the woods." Here Sweeney is shaving, as the orang-utan attempts to do in Poe's "The Murders in the Rue Morgue" (1841).

8. *The sickle motion . . . .:* description of an epileptic fit.

9. *Emerson:* said "an institution is the lengthened shadow of a man," in "Self-Reliance" (1841).

A COOKING EGG

Written 1919, first published in *Coterie*, London, May 1919.

1. *Title:* sense disputed. A cooking egg is an egg only good enough to be used in cooking; Grover Smith, *T. S. Eliot's Poetry and Plays: A Study in Sources and Meaning*, 3rd ed. (1960), p. 48, thinks it here applies to the speaker. Timothy Materer believes Eliot may have had in mind a passage in T. E. Hulme's "Romanticism and Classicism": "there is nothing particularly desirable about freshness *per se*. Works of arts aren't eggs . . ." ("A Note on T. S. Eliot's 'A Cooking Egg,' " *T. S. Eliot Review* [spring 1975]). Hulme's essay was not published until 1924, but Eliot had been introduced to Hulme by Pound and, being keenly interested in his ideas, might well have known the essay.

2. *Epigraph:* François Villon, *Le Grand Testament* (1489): "In the thirtieth year of my age, / When I have drunk down all my disgraces."

3. *Pipit:* in lines 1–8 probably a little girl. Suggestions include a retired nurse (denied by Eliot) and a former mistress; *sate* is a facetious archaism.

4. *Daguerreotypes:* daguerreotypy was a photographic method, introduced in 1839 and called after its French inventor, Louis Daguerre (1789–1851), which had a vogue in the 1840s (see Hawthorne's *The House of the Seven Gables*, 1851). The images could not be multiplied, and the process was soon superseded by early modern photography; Pipit's daguerreotypes therefore dated back to about 1850, and so, probably,

did her silhouettes, also a common mode of portraiture in the nineteenth century.

5. *An Invitation to the Dance:* This seems not to have been explained; it can hardly refer to Weber's composition of that name, which nobody would keep on a mantelpiece. A reproduction of some popular picture?

6. *want:* lack.

7. *For I shall meet . . . :* Sir Philip Sidney (1554–86), here subjected to a comic rhyme, was the Elizabethan model of honor. Eliot's interest in Shakespeare's *Coriolanus* was elsewhere more seriously expressed (see note 14 on *The Waste Land*).

8. *I shall not want:* perhaps remembering a letter of Ruskin's: "In heaven I mean to go and talk to Pythagoras and Socrates and Valerius Publicola" —as proposed by Grover Smith in *T. S. Eliot's Poetry and Plays*, p. 50.

9. *Sir Alfred Mond:* founder of Imperial Chemical Industries.

10. *Lucrezia Borgia:* Fifteenth-century Italian aristocrat and member of a family notorious for poisoning opponents.

11. *Madame Blavatsky:* Helena Petrovna Blavatsky (1831–91), founder of the Theosophical Society (1875). Its plan was "to collect and diffuse a knowledge of the laws which govern the universe," and her book *Isis Unveiled* (1877) was intended to further this plan. Despite a rather shady record she influenced W. B. Yeats, who was for a time a member of the Society.

12. *the Seven Sacred Trances:* Theosophist secret disciplines.

13. *Piccarda de Donati:* a nun who instructs Dante in heaven (*Paradiso,* iii).

14. *penny world:* a kind of nursery cake? (Not in *OED.*)

15. *Kentish Town . . . Golder's Green:* northern suburbs of London, the latter predominantly Jewish.

16. *Where are the eagles . . . :* Referring to defeated Roman armies, the trumpets attracting a derisive rhyme.

17. *A.B.C.s:* once numerous cheap London teashops belonging to the Aerated Bread Company.

LE DIRECTEUR

Written 1917, first published *Little Review,* July 1917. In *Poems* (1919) titled "Le Spectateur." Reverted to present title in the American edition of 1920.

1. "A plague on the wretched Thames, which flows so near *The Spectator.* The conservative director of *The Spectator* stinks. The reactionary shareholders of the conservative *Spectator* parade stealthily, arm in arm.

A pugnosed, ragged little girl in the gutter looks at the director of *The Spectator* and bursts with love."

Mélange Adultère de Tout

Written 1917, published with "Le Directeur." The title, "A Corrupt Mixture of Everything," is borrowed from a poem by Tristan Corbière.

1. "In America, a teacher; in England a journalist; you'll have to get a move on and sweat to follow my tracks. In Yorkshire, lecturer; in London a bit of a banker; you'll have trouble putting me down. In Paris I wear a don't-give-a-damn black cap. In Germany I am a philosopher, very excited by the love of mountaineering; I continually wander about, with many expressions of pleasure, from Damascus to Omaha. I will celebrate my birthday in an African oasis, clad in giraffe skin. They will display my cenotaph on the burning shores of Mozambique."

Lune de Miel ("Honeymoon")

Written 1917, published with the two preceding poems.

1. "They have seen the Netherlands and will return to Terre Haute. But one summer night, here they are at Ravenna, at their ease between two sheets, in the presence of hundreds of bedbugs. The summer sweat, and a strong odor of bitch. They lie on their backs, spreading their knees apart, four soft limbs swollen by bites. They lift the sheet the better to scratch. Only a short distance away is St. Apollinaire in Classe, a basilica well known to lovers of acanthus capitals, round which the wind swirls.

    "They're going to take the eight o'clock train to prolong their unhappiness from Padua to Milan, where the Last Supper is to be found, and a not-expensive restaurant. He thinks about tips, and keeps his accounts. They will have seen Switzerland and crossed France. And St. Apollinaire, gaunt and ascetic, an ancient factory for which God has lost his affection, still maintains, among his crumbling stones, the precise Byzantine form."

Saint Apollinaire/En Classe; Saint Apollinaire in Classe, a Byzantine church in Ravenna, famous for its murals.

The Hippopotamus

Written 1917, first published *Little Review* (Chicago), July 1917. It is a parody of or allusion to a poem by Théophile Gautier, "L'Hippopotame," which has nothing to do with the church. ("The big-bellied hippopotamus lives in the jungles of Java, where, from the back of each cave, there groan more monsters than one has ever dreamed of . . . wrapped in my conviction, a strong armour which nothing can penetrate, I go fearless through the desert.")

1. *Epigraph:* St. Ignatius' letter to the Trallians: "In the same way all should revere the deacons, and the Bishops, as Jesus Christ, the living son of the Father, commanded; and also the Priests, as the council of God and union of the Apostles. Without these the Church may not be so called, and what I urge upon you is what I myself believe." Ignatius (1st cent. C.E.) wrote in Greek, and the immediate source of this quotation is not known.

    And when . . .: Colossians 4:16. The Laodiceans were condemned as "lukewarm" in Revelation 3:15–16.

2. *Although he seems . . .:* distinguishing this hippopotamus from Gautier's.

3. *based upon a rock:* "Thou art Peter, and upon this rock I will build my church," Matt. 16:18 ("Peter" from Greek *petra,* rock).

4. *God . . . way:* William Cowper, "Light Shining out of Darkness" (1779): "God moves in a mysterious way His wonders to perform."

5. *Blood of the Lamb:* Revelation 7:14.

6. *miasmal:* relating to noxious exhalations.

DANS LE RESTAURANT

Written September 1918, first published *Little Review*, September 1918.

1. "The broken-down waiter who had nothing to do except scratch his fingers and lean on my shoulder [said]: 'In my part of the world it will be the rainy season—wind, hot sun, rain. It's what they call the beggar's washday.' (Garrulous, slobbery, round in the rump, I beg you at least not to dribble into the soup.) 'The willows were soaked and the buds on the brambles— It was there, taking shelter during a shower. I was seven, she was younger. She was quite wet and I gave her primroses.' The stains on his waistcoat added up to thirty-eight. 'I tickled her to make her laugh. She had a fresh smell, unknown to me.' [Later this line was replaced by: "and I experienced a moment of power and delight."]

    "But wait a moment, you old lecher, at that age . . . 'Sir, the outcome is sad. A large dog came, to curry favor with us; I was afraid and left her in midcourse. It's a shame.' So then you have your vulture! Go away and scrape off the wrinkles in your face. Here's my fork, scrub your skull. What right have you to pay the cost of your experiences as I do? Here's ten sous for the bathhouse. [The remainder of this poem is loosely translated as "Death by Water" (*Waste Land*, IV).] Phlebas the Phoenician, a fortnight drowned, forgot the cries of the gulls and the Cornish swell, and the profits and the losses, and the cargo of tin. A current under the sea carried him far away, returning him to the stages of his former life. Think then, it was a wretched fate; however, he was once a fine tall man."

2. *vautour:* vulture. His shame at running away from the dog returns daily to torture him, like the vulture that ate the liver of Prometheus.

WHISPERS OF IMMORTALITY

Written 1918, first published *Little Review* (Chicago), September 1918.

1. *Webster:* John Webster (ca. 1582–ca. 1625), one of the Jacobean dramatists who greatly interested Eliot at this period, an interest here reconciled with his passion for the poetry of Baudelaire, Gautier, and Laforgue. Webster's tragedies are violent, lustful, and death-obsessed.

2. *Daffodil bulbs . . .:* cf. Webster, *The White Devil*, V.iv, where the ghost of Brachiano enters ("in his hand a pot of lily-flowers, with a skull in it") and shows the skull to Flamineo, who exclaims, "A dead man's skull beneath the roots of flowers!" (line 142).

3. *Donne:* John Donne (1572–1631), for several years an exemplary poet for Eliot, who admired the union of thought and feeling in his poetry; the reference is also to Donne the preacher, perhaps especially to his last sermon, "Death's Duel," a macabre evocation of mortality.

4. *Grishkin:* alluding to the Russian ballet dancer Serafima Astafieva (1876–1934), to whom Ezra Pound introduced Eliot, but also referring to Gautier's "Carmen" (*Emaux et camées* [*Enamels and Cameos*], 1863): "Carmen est maigre—un trait de bistre / Cerne son oeil de gitana" ("Carmen is thin— / A line of bistre makes a ring under her eyes").

5. *pneumatic bliss:* Alluding, as Pound noted, to "Grishkin's Dunlop tyre boozum."

6. *Abstract Entities:* concepts like numbers and universals, as distinguished from empirical objects. On the other hand, the poets ("our lot") have not the consolation of the empirical pneumatic bust, but have to resort to skull and skeleton.

MR. ELIOT'S SUNDAY MORNING SERVICE

Written 1918, first published *Little Review* (Chicago), September 1918.

1. *Epigraph:* Marlowe, *The Jew of Malta*, IV.i.21.
2. *Polyphiloprogenitive:* Producing many children (or ideas). *OED* ii gives this as the first use of the word, but under *philoprogenitive* cites several nineteenth-century examples.
3. *sapient sutlers:* wiseacre provision agents.
4. *In the beginning . . . .:* John 1:1.
5. *Superfetation:* multiple impregnation. τὸ ἕν [Greek] to en: "the One."
6. *mensual:* recurring monthly (the relevance is not clear).
7. *enervate Origen:* Origen of Alexandria (ca. 185–254 C.E.) was one of the greatest and most prolific of theologians and Bible scholars. He took literally Matthew 19:12 ("there be eunuchs, which have made themselves eunuchs for the kingdom of heaven's sake") and castrated himself. "Enervate" is an obsolete word for "emasculated."
8. *Umbrian school:* painters of this central Italian district, particularly in the fifteenth century, for example Piero della Francesca. Eliot may have had in mind Piero's *Baptism*, in the National Gallery, London.
9. *gesso:* plaster used to prepare a canvas for painting.
10. *Paraclete:* the Comforter; the Holy Spirit, represented as a dove.
11. *presbyters:* priests.
12. *piaculative:* the word exists nowhere else; "piacular" means "expiatory," "a sacrifice made in pursuit of pardon."
13. *invisible and dim:* cf. Henry Vaughan, "The Night": "O for that night! Where I in him / Might live invisible and dim."
14. *the bees . . . epicene:* the bees are "epicene," a Greek derivative meaning common to both (sexes or genders) and so applied to whatever has characteristics of both sexes; bees carry pollen from the male stamen to the female pistil.
15. *Polymath:* learned in many fields.

SWEENEY AMONG THE NIGHTINGALES

Written 1918, first published *Little Review* (Chicago), September 1918. "Nightingales" is said also to have the slang sense of "prostitutes."

1. *Epigraph:* "Alas, I have been struck deep a deadly wound" (Aeschylus, *Agamemnon*). In *Ara Vos Prec* the poem has another epigraph: "Why should I speak of the nightingale? The nightingale sings of adulterate wrong," from *The Raigne of King Edward the Third*, II.i.109–110

(ca. 1595), now often attributed, in whole or part, to Shakespeare. The allusion is to the myth of Philomela's rape by Tereus. She was transformed into a nightingale and sang her complaint.

2. *maculate:* spotted (with implication of impurity).

3. *Raven:* the southern constellation Corvus (according to *OED* ii, obsolete and rare).

4. *the hornèd gate:* in classical legend the gate through which true dreams pass; false dreams enter by the gate of ivory.

5. *Gloomy Orion:* Orion is a bright constellation, but Marlowe, *Dido, Queen of Carthage* (1594), I.ii.26, takes Virgil's idea that it was clouded over. *The Dog:* Sirius, the dog star.

6. *Rachel née Rabinovitch:* Christopher Ricks (*T. S. Eliot and Prejudice* [1988], p. 31) observes that this is an abnormal usage; the usual formula inserts the married name of the woman before "née." The name is Jewish.

7. *murderous paws:* cf. *Dido, Queen of Carthage*, II.i.512, "murdering paws."

8. Eliot explained that he had in mind Sophocles, *Oedipus at Colonus*, in which the king reaches the end of his life in a grove of the Furies where many nightingales sing. He transfers this to the scene of the murder of Agamemnon. Eliot first wrote "droppings" but accepted Pound's suggestion of "siftings."

THE WASTE LAND

For the longer manuscript Eliot submitted to Pound (it was entitled *He Do the Police in Different Voices*, from Dickens, *Our Mutual Friend*, chapter 16) see Valerie Eliot, ed., *T. S. Eliot: The Waste Land: A Facsmile and Transcript of the Original Drafts including the Annotations of Ezra Pound* (1971). This version was much longer than the poem published in 1922. Parts had been written "about 1914 or even earlier" (*Waste Land MS*, p. 130). On 5 November, 1919, Eliot wrote, "I hope to get started on a poem I have in mind" (Valerie Eliot, ed., *The Letters of T. S. Eliot* [1988], p. 343). The work was "partly on paper" by 9 May 1921 (*Letters*, p. 451). In September of that year Eliot's health broke down. He sought rest and recovery first at Margate, on the coast east of London, and then at Lausanne, Switzerland, continuing work on the poem. In January 1922 he was with Pound, corrector of his manuscript, in Paris. On 11 June Eliot read the poem to Leonard and Virginia Woolf. It appeared in the first number of

Eliot's new periodical *The Criterion* in October (without the notes) and was reprinted in *The Dial* in the following month. In December 1922 Boni & Liveright (New York) published the poem as a book of sixty-four pages with the addition of a series of notes (intended to swell a very short book). The first English book publication was by Leonard and Virginia Woolf at their Hogarth Press in Richmond, Surrey, September 1923. The dedication to Ezra Pound (*il miglior fabbro*, "the better craftsman") was absent from these first printings. Eliot wrote it in ink to the copy of the Boni & Liveright edition presented to Pound, and it was added to the printed version in the London *Poems, 1909–1925* (1925).

1. *Epigraph:* "For I myself once saw with my own eyes the Sibyl hanging in a cage, and when the boys asked her, 'Sybil, what do you want?' she answered 'I want to die.' " This is one of the tall stories of Tri-malchio in the *Satyricon* of Petronius Arbiter, a first-century novel of which substantial fragments survive. The Sibyl was granted immor-tality but not youth. This epigraph replaced one from Conrad's *Heart of Darkness*, which Eliot dropped on Pound's advice.

I. THE BURIAL OF THE DEAD

1. *April:* usually the month of Easter, or rebirth.
2. *Starnbergersee:* a lake south of Munich, which Eliot visited in 1911. It was the site of King Ludwig's castle, Schloss Berg. He was Wagner's patron; for an argument connecting him with Wagner in this poem see Herbert Knust, *Wagner, the King, and "The Waste Land"* (1967).
3. *Hofgarten:* a park in Munich.
4. *Bin gar . . .:* "I'm not Russian at all, I come from Lithuania, pure German." G. K. L. Morris in 1950 made the chance discovery that this episode may derive in part from the memoirs of Countess Marie von Wallersee, published in 1913. Later it emerged that Eliot was acquainted with the countess, who was related to the mad King Lud-wig II of Bavaria (Wagner's patron) and to several archdukes. Valerie Eliot (*Waste Land MS.*, p. 126) explains that line 12 was remembered from a conversation with the countess. For elaborate interpretation of the significance of the passage, see Kunst. The countess believed in fortune-telling by cards. She was murdered at Lake Leman (see line 182).
5. *Son of man:* Ezekiel 2:1.
6. *broken images:* Ezekiel 6:4.
7. *the cricket . . .:* see page [ms. 67]. Eliot's note refers to Ecclesiastes 13:5,

the great lament for old age: "The grasshopper shall be a burden, and desire shall fail. . . ."

8. *There is shadow . . .:* these lines are a later version of lines in Eliot's early poem "The Death of Saint Narcissus" (ca. 1915), not published until 1950:

> *Come under the shadow of this gray rock—*
> *Come in under the shadow of this gray rock,*
> *And I will show you something different from either*
> *Your shadow sprawling over the sand at daybreak, or*
> *Your shadow leaping behind the fire against the red rock:*
> *I will show you his bloody cloth and limbs*
> *And the gray shadow on his lips.*

The manuscript of this poem was included in the batch Eliot gave to Pound. It had earlier been set in type, with some variants, in *Poetry* (Chicago) but withdrawn before publication (*Waste Land MS*, p. 129).

9. *A handful of dust:* this phrase, which occurred earlier in Donne, Tennyson and Conrad, gave Evelyn Waugh the title of his novel (1934).

10. *Frisch weht . . .:* "Fresh blows the wind to the homeland. My Irish child, why do you delay?" The song sung by a sailor at the beginning of Wagner's *Tristan und Isolde* (1865).

11. *hyacinths:* symbols of resurrection.

12. *I could not / Speak . . .:* a moment of mystical recognition (and subsequent failure); Pound wanted him to change this, but Eliot declined.

13. "Waste and empty the sea." Spoken by a shepherd at the beginning of *Tristan und Isolde*, Act III, as he scans the horizon for signs of Isolde's ship. (Eliot, who had been greatly moved by the opera when a student in Paris, shared in the wave of enthusiasm for Wagner in early-twentieth-century England; see the works of George Moore and D. H. Lawrence, who, however, disliked *Tristan*, finding it pornographic). Isolde's eventual arrival is followed by Tristan's virtually self-inflicted death.

14. *Madame Sosostris:* probably borrowed from Aldous Huxley's novel *Chrome Yellow* (1921), in which a guest at a house party pretends to be a fortune-teller, Madame Sosostris.

15. *pack of cards:* the Tarot pack, usually of seventy-eight cards. Eliot's note says he was "not familiar with the exact constitution of the Tarot pack of cards," so he made them up when he needed to. He adds that the Hanged Man is a member of the traditional pack, here associated with the Hanged God of Sir James Frazer and the hooded

figure in Part V. Belladonna and the Phoenician Sailor (representing the fertility god supposed to have been thrown into the sea at the end of summer) are invented cards, but the Man with Three Staves is authentic, though Eliot arbitrarily associates him with the Fisher King. The original magical function of the pack was lost, and it degenerated into fortune-telling for amusement. For the idea that the Tarot pack is related to fertility rituals, see Jessie L. Weston, *From Ritual to Romance* (1920).

16. *Those are pearls . . . :* Shakespeare, *The Tempest*, I.ii.401; Ariel is telling Ferdinand that his father has drowned and been transfigured.

17. *Lady of the Rocks:* ironical reference to Leonardo's painting *Madonna of the Rocks.*

18. *one-eyed:* because seen in profile.

19. *Unreal City . . . flowed:* indebted to Baudelaire, "Les Sept Vieillards" ("The Seven Old Men"): "Fourmillante cité, cité pleine de rêves, / Où le spectre en plein jour raccroche le passant" ("swarming city, where in broad daylight the ghost accosts the passer-by"). Eliot's admiration for Baudelaire was founded in part on his originality as the poet of the modern city. Quoting these lines in "What Dante Means to Me," a talk given in 1950 (reprinted in *To Criticize the Critic*, 1965, pp. 125–135, Eliot says "A great poet can give a younger poet everything that he has to give him, in a very few lines," and quotes these lines as an example of what he means.

20. *so many . . . so many:* Dante, *Inferno*, III.55–57: "sì lunga tratta di gente, ch'io non avrei mai creduto / che morte tanta n'avesse disfatta" ("so long a stream of people that I should never have believed that death had undone so many") (Eliot's note). In Dante these are the spirits who in life knew neither good nor evil; see Eliot's essay on Baudelaire (*Selected Essays*, pp. 381ff.).

21. *Sighs . . . exhaled:* Dante, *Inferno*, IV.25–27: "Quivi, secondo che per ascoltare, non avea pianto, ma' che di sospiri, che l'aura eterna facevan tremare" ("Here, to my hearing, there was no lamentation except sighs, which caused the eternal air to tremble") (Eliot's note). Dante is in the limbo of the unbaptized.

22. *And each man . . . :* Dante, *Inferno*, XXXIV.15: "altro, com'arco, il volto a' piedi inverte" ("another, like a bow, bends his face to his feet").

23. *St. Mary Woolnoth:* City of London church, by Nicholas Hawksmoore (1661–1736), built 1716–27. It is in the heart of the financial district and close to the poet's workplace.

24. *dead sound:* Eliot says he was familiar with this phenomenon, which

would recur daily as the workers were reaching their offices at 9 A.M.

25. *Mylae:* a battle in the first Punic War (260 B.C.E.) between the Romans and the Carthaginians, fought for control of Mediterranean trade.

26. *O keep . . . again:* in Webster's *The White Devil* Cornelia, referring to "the friendless bodies of unburied men," sings a dirge: "But keep the wolf far hence that's foe to men / For with his nails he'll dig them up again" (V.iv.118–119). Possibly an allusion to the English passion for dogs. Eliot had more allusions to Webster in the draft of the poem.

27. *You! . . . mon frère!:* from Baudelaire's Preface to *Les Fleurs du mal* (*The Flowers of Evil*), 1857: "You! Hypocrite reader! my likeness, my brother!"

II. A Game of Chess

1. Referring to Middleton's play *Women Beware Women* (ca. 1621). In act 2, scene 2 the Duke's procuress plays chess with a girl's mother while the Duke is seducing the girl upstairs; the chess moves are made to correspond to his progress.

2. *The Chair . . . throne: Antony and Cleopatra,* II.ii.195ff.: "The barge she sat in, like a burnished throne / Burned on the water." Eliot refers to this passage, but may also be thinking of *Cymbeline,* II.ii and iv, and of Keats's *Lamia.* The extreme luxury is an ironical setting for the scene of hysteria and ennui.

3. *laquearia:* paneled ceiling; Eliot refers us to Virgil, *Aeneid,* I.726, in which, at a banquet given by Dido for Aeneas, "flaming torches hang from the gold-paneled ceiling and conquer the night with their flames."

4. *the sylvan scene:* Milton, *Paradise Lost,* IV.140 (Eliot's note).

5. *The change of Philomel:* Philomel was raped by Tereus, the husband of her sister Procne, and had her tongue cut out. She was changed into a nightingale (Ovid, *Metamorphoses,* VI) (Eliot's note).

6. Eliot's note refers the reader to the return of the Philomel theme at line 204.

7. *pursues:* note the change of tense.

8. *"Jug, jug":* the nightingale's sound as represented in Elizabethan poetry.

9. Eliot's note refers the reader to line 195, where the rats return.

10. *The wind under the door:* Eliot refers to Webster, *The Devil's Law Case,* III.ii: "Sits the wind in that door still?"

11. *Those are pearls . . . .: The Tempest,* I.ii.398. Eliot's note refers back to line 48 and also, mysteriously, to line 37.

12. O O O O . . .: This is adapted from a song in a Broadway show, Ziegfeld's *Follies of 1912*; Eliot added the O's and the intrusive "he" in Shakespeare's name. He is imitating ragtime.

13. *a game of chess:* here Eliot refers to the passage in *Women Beware Women* (see note on title). In Middleton's play the chess accompanies sexual activity; here it seems to be a substitute for it. Copying the poem much later, Eliot here inserted another line, which had been omitted at the request of Vivienne Eliot: "The ivory men make company between us."

14. *demobbed:* demobilized (released from army service).

15. *HURRY UP . . .:* the public houses had licenced hours, and drinkers were warned when closing time approached.

16. *four years:* i.e., for the duration of the war of 1914–18.

17. This line was supplied by Vivienne Eliot.

18. *bring it off:* induce abortion.

19. *chemist:* pharmacist.

20. *gammon:* ham.

21. *Good night, ladies:* Hamlet, IV.v.73; Ophelia's last words.

III. THE FIRE SERMON

1. A sermon preached by Buddha against the fires of lust and other passions.

2. *Sweet Thames . . .:* Spenser, "Prothalamion" (refrain), where the river and its nymphs celebrate a noble wedding. Now the river has become a scene of litter and loveless seduction.

3. *loitering:* recalling Keats, "La Belle Dame Sans Merci," line 2.

4. *By the waters of Leman . . .:* "By the waters of Babylon there we sat down, yea, we wept, when we remembered Zion" (Psalms, 137.1). Leman is Lake Geneva, where Eliot worked on the poem (at Lausanne). There is possibly an allusion to Jean-Jacques Rousseau's remarks on his having sat weeping beside Lake Geneva. "Leman" is also an old word for "mistress."

5. *But at my back . . .:* Parodying Marvell, "To His Coy Mistress," lines 21–22: "But at my back I always hear / Time's winged chariot hurrying near."

6. *the king my brother's wreck:* Eliot refers to *The Tempest*, I.ii.393: "Sitting upon a bank, / Weeping again the King my father's wrack, / This music crept by me upon the waters, / Allaying both their fury and my passion. . . ." See line 257.

7. *But at my back . . .:* Marvell, "To His Coy Mistress," line 21.

8. *The sound . . . soda water:* Eliot refers to John Day, *The Parliament of*

Bees: "When of the sudden, listening, you shall hear / A noise of horns and hunting, which shall bring / Actaeon to Diana in the spring, / Where all shall see her naked skin." Actaeon surprised Diana when she was bathing, and for punishment was turned into a stag and hunted down by his own hounds; an old allegorical reading took this to signify the destruction of men by their own intemperate desires. Sweeney is Eliot's natural man; his leman is called Mrs. Porter, perhaps for the rhyme. Eliot said he did not know the origin of the ballad from which he took the lines; "it was reported to me from Sydney, Australia." The ballad was well known to the Australian soldiers of World War I, usually in more obscene versions. Eliot's predilection for such songs is now illustrated by the bawdy verses printed by Ricks, pp. 305ff.

9. *Et . . . coupole*: from Verlaine's sonnet "Parsifal": And O, these children's voices singing in the dome!" Verlaine's reference is to the choir of children near the end of Wagner's opera *Parsifal*, when Parsifal's feet are ceremonially washed before he proceeds to the Grail, the sick king is healed, and the wasteland is restored. On this passage see J. S. Brooker and J. Bentley, *Reading the Waste Land* (1990), pp. 135–6.

10. *Twit twit . . . Tereu*: Cf. the nightingale's song in John Lyly (1554–1606), *Alexander and Campaspe*: "Tis the ravished nightingale; / Jug. jug. jug. jug. tereu, she cries." (The author may not be Lyly.) *Tereu* is the vocative form of the Greek *Tereus*.

11. *Unreal City*: A return to the commercial scene and an encounter deriving from Eliot's own experience.

12. *Eugenides . . . merchant*: the name suggests (ironically) that the merchant comes of good family. Smyrna in Turkey was a source of currants. Some commentators remind us that currants are shriveled grapes, hence dried-up fertility symbols.

13. *C.i.f.*: "The currants were quoted at a price 'carriage and insurance free to London'; and the Bill of Lading, etc., were to be handed to the buyer upon payment of the sight draft" (Eliot's note). This explanation is said (by Southam, *A Student's Guide to the Selected Poems of T. S. Eliot*, 6th ed., 1994, p. 170) to be incorrect; c.i.f. means "cost, insurance and freight."

14. *demotic*: colloquial. Eliot first wrote "abominable"; "demotic" is Pound's suggestion.

15. *Cannon Street Hotel*: hotel in the City of London (where, as it happened, Wagner stayed when he arrived in London with the libretto

of *Parsifal*). It was a useful meeting place for foreign and London businessmen.

16. *Metropole:* Grand hotel at Brighton, on the south coast some sixty miles from London; Brighton was famous for weekend assignations.

17. *At the violet hour . . . :* lines 215–56 were originally written in quatrains, but when Pound deleted some of the lines Eliot made no attempt to retrieve that arrangement.

18. *Tiresias:* see Eliot's note. The Latin of Ovid describes the sex change of Tiresias. Tiresias had struck two copulating snakes and been turned into a woman; later he struck another such pair, and was turned back into a man. Jupiter tells Juno that he believes women to have more pleasure in sex than men have; she disagrees, and they decide to consult Tiresias, who has been both man and woman. He agrees with Jupiter, and Juno, in anger, blinds him. To compensate him Jupiter gives Tiresias the gift of prophecy. Broadly speaking, Tiresias is the point of view from which the exemplars of waste-land degeneracy are seen to meet.

19. *sailor . . . sea:* Eliot's note indicates that he is imitating a fragment by the Greek poetess Sappho (7th cent. B.C.E.): she prays to the evening star, which brings "the sheep, the goat, and the child back to the mother" (*Fragment* 149). Eliot is also remembering Robert Louis Stevenson's "Requiem": "Home is the sailor, home from sea, and the hunter home from the hill."

20. *Bradford:* Yorkshire wool town; fortunes were said to have been made there during the First World War.

21. *Tiresias:* see note 18 above. He is the blind prophet in Sophocles' *Oedipus Rex*. He knows about the king's incest and parricide, which brought the plague on Thebes.

22. *foresuffered all:* i.e., such loveless sexual encounters, both as man and as woman.

23. *walked . . . dead:* Odysseus consulted Tiresias in the underworld (Homer, *Odyssey*, XI).

24. *When . . . folly:* the song in Goldsmith's *Vicar of Wakefield* (1766): "When lovely woman stoops to folly, / And finds too late that men betray, / What charm can soothe her melancholy, / What art can wash her guilt away? // The only art her guilt to cover, / To hide her shame from every eye, / To give repentance to her lover / And wring his bosom—is to die."

25. *This music . . . :* see lines 48, 125.

26. *Strand:* a street running east and west, parallel to the Thames, and

connecting the City of London with Westminster. *Queen Victoria Street:* in the City.

27. *Lower Thames Street:* near the Thames at London Bridge.

28. *fishmen:* workers at Billingsgate Fish Market.

29. *Magnus Martyr . . . gold:* St. Magnus Martyr is a church by the great architect Sir Christopher Wren (1671-6) with a fine interior, much admired by Eliot. The church had recently been redecorated.

30. *The river sweats:* here begins what Eliot called "the song of the three Thames-daughters," imitating, as he says, the three Rhine-daughters of Wagner's *Ring*. In the last of the four operas the Rhine-maidens flirt with Siegfried but lament the theft of the gold of the Nibelungs and the destruction of the old world of the gods. The refrain here is the same as that of the Rhine-maidens. Eliot admired Conrad's *Heart of Darkness*, which begins on a lower reach of the Thames. Pound had vetoed Eliot's wish to use Conrad's "The horror! The horror," Kurtz's words near the end of Conrad's novel.

31. *Greenwich reach:* the river at Greenwich, east of London.

32. *The Isle of Dogs:* the riverbank opposite Greenwich, at the time a poor district in contrast to the magnificence of Wren's great Greenwich Hospital on the other side.

33. *Elizabeth and Leicester:* Eliot's note refers to Froude's *History of England*, VII, which describes the pair flirting on a barge; she entertained Leicester at Greenwich House.

34. *Trams . . . trees:* a return to the modern scene.

35. *Highbury . . . Undid me:* Dante, *Purgatorio*, V.134: "Siena mi fe, disfecemi Maremma" ("Siena made me, Maremma undid me"). Spoken by La Pia of Siena, whose husband murdered her at Maremma. Highbury is a northern suburb; Richmond and Kew are popular riverside resorts on the river to the west.

36. *Moorgate:* City area, east London.

37. *Margate:* A seaside resort near London. Eliot spent a month there October–November 1921 trying to recover from the breakdown of his health, and working on *The Waste Land*.

38. *To Carthage then I came:* from St. Augustine's *Confessions*, III.i: "to Carthage then I came, where a cauldron of unholy loves sang all about my ears." Augustine is describing the city's assault on his senses in the years before his conversion.

39. *Burning . . . :* Eliot refers to the Buddha's Fire Sermon. It condemns the senses, which introduce the soul to a world of fire, and hinder its liberation from desire.

40. *O Lord thou pluckest me out:* Augustine, *Confessions:* "I entangle my steps with these outward beauties, but thou pluckest me out, O Lord, thou pluckest me out!" Eliot remarks that the collocation of Eastern and Western asceticism "is not an accident." Both pray for release from enslavement to sense, particularly sex.

IV. DEATH BY WATER

1. See note on "Dans le Restaurant," and line 55. These lines, written, like V, when Eliot was in a clinic at Lausanne (November–December 1921) are adapted from the last seven in Eliot's French poem "Dans le Restaurant" (1918), here translated: "Phlebas the Phoenician, two weeks drowned, forgot the cries of the gulls and the swell of Cornish seas, and the profit and the loss, and the cargo of tin: an undersea current carried him very far, taking him back through the stages of his former life. Think of it, it was a hard fate; he was after all once handsome and tall." Pound insisted on the retention of this section; the manuscript contains a long nautical poem of which these lines form the conclusion. Pound admired the lines for their own sake, but saw their connection with Mr. Eugenides and the quotations from *The Tempest.* In any case, death by water is a recurring theme in the poem.

V. WHAT THE THUNDER SAID

Eliot is known to have written this section in a state that might be called inspired; he set it down almost without a blot, and it appeared in print with very little change. It survived Pound's surgery intact. Eliot thought it "the best part" and the part that justified the whole. He specifies three themes in the first part (lines 322–94): the journey to Emmaus; the approach to the Chapel Perilous; the decay of Eastern Europe. For the Emmaus journey see Luke 24:13–31, in which the resurrected Jesus joins two disciples on the road to Emmaus and they do not recognize him. The Chapel Perilous is the final stage of the Grail quest, described by Jessie L. Weston. The third reference is to the chaos of Eastern Europe in the aftermath of World War I, especially the success of the Bolsheviks.

1. *After the torchlight . . . .:* lines 322–28 allude to events from the betrayal of Christ to his death.

2. *hermit-thrush:* Eliot's note gives details (taken from a book he had acquired in his youth) about this North American bird, whose song, he says, is "justly celebrated."

3. *the third . . . you:* Eliot explains that the inspiration of lines 360–66 was the account of Sir Ernest Shackleton, the Antarctic explorer, of the delusion suffered by exhausted men "that there was *one more member* than could actually be counted." Here this is related to the experiences of the disciples on the road to Emmaus.

4. *What is that sound . . . Unreal:* lines 367–77. Eliot quotes Hermann Hesse's *Glimpse into Chaos* (1920): "Half of Europe, half of eastern Europe at least, is already on its way into chaos, reeling drunkenly in sacred madness along the edge of the abyss, singing drunkenly and ecstatically as Dmitri Karamazov sang. The bourgeois laughs resentfully at these songs, the saint and seer hears them and weeps." (Translation courtesy of Sheila Stern.) The reference must be mainly to the Russian Revolution, but the tone is apocalyptic, and Eliot might have had in mind a prophecy that one sign of the end would be the movement westward of eastern hordes.

5. *A woman . . . :* 378ff. This phantasmagorical interlude owes something to Surrealism and to the painter Hieronymus Bosch (ca. 1450–ca. 1516). It continues the theme of apocalyptic terror and looks forward to the horrors that test the knight at the Chapel Perilous.

6. *cisterns:* in Richard Strauss's opera *Salome* (1905) John the Baptist sings out of the cistern in which he is imprisoned.

7. *the chapel:* the Chapel Perilous of medieval romance, where the resolution of the initiate was tested.

8. *co co rico co co rico:* the cock's cry is given in the French style; it may reflect the crowing of the cock in *Hamlet* I.i, and seems to announce rain.

9. *Ganga:* the Ganges, the sacred river of India.

10. *Himavant:* holy mountain in the Himalayas.

11. *DA:* in the holy book *Brihadaranyaka-Upanishad*, referred to by Eliot, gods, demons, and men ask the Creator to speak to them; he replies "DA" to each group, and each interprets it differently, using the three Sanskrit words employed in the following lines (402, 412, 419): "give," "sympathize," "control."

12. *spider:* Eliot refers to Webster, *The White Devil*, V.vi.156–8: "they'll remarry / Ere the worm pierce your winding sheet, ere the spider / Make a thin curtain for your epitaphs." "They" refers to women in general.

13. *the key:* Eliot refers to Dante, *Inferno*, XXXIII.46: "ed io sentii chiavar l'uscio di sotto / all'orribile torre" ("and from below I heard the door of the horrible tower being locked"). The words are spoken by Ug-

olino, who devoured his children when starving in captivity. The key of the tower was thrown into the river. Eliot adds to this image of suffering isolation a quotation from the work of a philosopher he had intensively studied as a Ph.D. student, F. H. Bradley's *Appearance and Reality* (1893), p. 346. Eliot's note offers an important clue to what he is doing in such poems as "Gerontion" and *The Waste Land*.

14. *Coriolanus:* Eliot greatly admired Shakespeare's play of this title (ca. 1608) and later wrote the unfinished poem "Coriolan" (the title of Beethoven's overture), first published in 1936. Coriolanus was broken and exiled through his own pride and unwillingness to ingratiate himself with the mob; he revived—for a moment—when given the chance to fight against Rome, his own country.

15. *controlling hands:* Eliot, a good sailor in his youth, chooses the management of a boat as an image of control, transferring it at once to a personal figure: you *would* have responded in the same way.

16. *I sat . . . Fishing:* Eliot's note [p. 75] refers to Jessie Weston's chapter on the Fisher King. the speaker is the Fisher King.

17. *Shall I . . .:* "Thus saith the Lord, Set thine house in order: for thou shalt die and not live" (Isaiah 38:1).

18. *London . . . down:* an English nursery rhyme.

19. *Poi . . . affina:* Eliot refers to Dante, *Purgatorio*, XXVI.148: " 'Ara vos prec, per aquella valor / que vos guida al som de l'escalina, / sovegna vos a temps de ma dolor.' / Poi s'ascose nel foco che gli affina" (" 'Now, I pray you, by that virtue / which leads you to the top of the stair, / think of me in my time of pain.' / Then he hid himself in the refining fire"). The speaker is the Provençal poet Arnaut Daniel, using his own language. The passage was especially dear to Eliot, who titled his third book of verse *Ara Vos Prec*, and wrote admiringly of the passage in his essay on Dante (1929).

20. *Quando fiam ceu chelidon:* "When shall I become like a swallow?" From the *Pervigilium Veneris* ("The Vigil of Venus"), an anonymous poem written between the second and fifth centuries C.E., dealing with Venus and the spring. It tells the story of Philomel and Tereus. Philomel's sister Procne was turned into a swallow. *O swallow, swallow:* cf. Tennyson, *The Princess*, IV. In later editions *ceu* was replaced by *uti*, but the sense is the same.

21. *Le prince . . . abolie:* "The prince of Aquitaine in the ruined tower." From Gérard de Nerval's sonnet "El Deschidado" ("The Disinherited"). Nerval (1808–55) refers to himself as the disinherited prince. The troubadour poets were associated with the castles of Aquitaine

in southern France. A Tarot card shows a tower struck by lightning.

22. *These fragments . . . .:* The Spanish Tragedy, to which Eliot refers, is a play by Thomas Kyd (1557?–95) subtitled *Hieronymo's Mad Again.* Hieronymo, seeking revenge for the murder of his son, takes the opportunity offered by an invitation to stage a court entertainment, saying, "Why then, I'll fit you," meaning both "I'll give you what you want" and "I'll give you your due." He contrives the murder of the guilty in the course of a play supposed to be written in Latin, Greek, Italian, and French, but "thought good to be set down in English, more largely, for the easier understanding to every public reader" (IV.iv.18–19). Eliot, as it were, retains the original languages.

23. *shantih shantih shantih:* explained by Eliot, when repeated as it is here, as a formal ending to an Upanishad (commentary on the Hindu scriptures). " 'The peace which passeth understanding' [Philippians 4:7] is our equivalent to this word."

NOTES ON THE WASTE LAND

1. Eliot added these notes to the New York edition published by Boni & Liveright in December 1922, apparently at the request of Liveright, who wanted to bulk out the volume. "The notes to *The Waste Land!* I had intended at first only to put down all the references for my quotations, with a view to spiking the guns of critics of my earlier poems who had accused me of plagiarism. Then, when it came to print *The Waste Land* as a little book . . . it was discovered that the poem was inconveniently short, so I set to work to expand the notes, in order to provide a few more pages of printed matter, with the result that they became the remarkable exposition of bogus scholarship that is still on view today. I have sometimes thought of getting rid of these notes; but now they can never be unstuck. They have had almost greater popularity than the poem itself—anyone who bought my book of poems, and found that the Notes to *The Waste Land* were not in it, would demand his money back. . . . My notes stimulated the wrong kind of interest among the seekers of sources. It was just, no doubt, that I should pay my tribute to the work of Miss Jessie Weston; but I regret having sent so many enquirers off on a wild goose chase after Tarot cards and the Holy Grail" ("The Frontiers of Criticism" (1956), in T. S. Eliot, *On Poetry and Poets* (1957), pp. 109–10).

   Translations, where needed, are supplied above in the notes of this edition.